Celebrating

VIETNAMESE
SOUL FOOD

The publisher wishes to thank the staff at **Mai Vietnamese Cuisine** for their assistance throughout the photography session, and **Sia Huat Pte Ltd** for the loan and use of their tableware.

Editor: Lydia Leong
Art Direction: Ang Lee Ming
Designer: Andrew Tan
Photographer: Charlie Lim

© 2004 Marshall Cavendish International (Asia) Private Limited

Published by Marshall Cavendish Cuisine
An imprint of Marshall Cavendish International (Asia) Private Limited
A member of Times Publishing Limited
Times Centre, 1 New Industrial Road, Singapore 536196
Tel: (65) 6213 9288   Fax: (65) 6285 4871
E-mail: te@sg.marshallcavendish.com
Online Bookstore: www.marshallcavendish.com/genref

Malaysian Office:
Federal Publications Sdn Berhad (General & Reference Publishing) (3024-D)
Times Subang, Lot 46, Persiaran Teknologi Subang,
Subang Hi-Tech Industrial Park
Batu Tiga, 40000 Shah Alam, Selangor Darul Ehsan, Malaysia
Tel: (603) 5635 2191   Fax: (603) 5635 2706
E-mail: cchong@tpg.com.my

All rights reserved. No part of this publication may be reproduced, stored in a retrieval system or transmitted, in any form or by any means, electronic, mechanical, photocopying, recording or otherwise, without the prior permission of the copyright owner.

National Library Board (Singapore) Cataloguing in Publication Data

Ha Mai,- 1968-
Vietnamese soul food /- Ha Mai. – Singapore :- Marshall Cavendish Cuisine,- c2004.
p. cm.
ISBN : 981-232-934-X

1. Cookery, Vietnamese. I. Title.

TX724.5.V5
641.59597 – dc21   SLS2004102535

Printed in Singapore by Times Printers Pte Ltd

To my mother who taught me the basics of Vietnamese cooking.

CONTENTS

Preface   6

Soups & Noodles
Pork Cabbage Roll Soup
   (*Canh Bap Cai Cuon Thit*)   8
Minced Beef and Tomato Soup
   (*Canh Bo Rau Ram*)   8

Tamarind Fish Soup (*Canh Chua Ca*)   10
Tomato and Egg Soup (*Canh Ca Chua Trung*) 10

Pig's Trotters Noodle Soup
   (*Banh Canh Gio Heo*)   12
Fish Tomato Soup (*Canh Ca Nau Ngot*)   12

Bitter Gourd Stuffed with Minced Pork Soup
   (*Canh Kho Qua Nhoi Thit*)   14
Chicken Glass Noodle Soup (*Mien Ga*)   14

Crab Noodle Soup (*Bun Rieu*)   16
Chicken Noodle Soup (*Pho Ga*)   16

Grilled Pork with Vermicelli (*Bun Thit Nuong*)   18
Hanoi Chicken Vermicelli (*Bun Thang*)   18

Hue-styled Spicy Beef and Pork Noodles
   (*Bun Bo Hue*)   20
Beef Noodle Soup (*Pho Bo*)   20

Handiwork Dishes
Net Spring Rolls (*Cha Gio Re*)   22
Golden Spring Rolls (*Cha Gio*)   22

Crispy Chicken Wings with Fish Sauce
   (*Canh Ga Chien Nuoc Mam*)   24
Saigon Pancake (*Banh Xeo*)   24

Sugarcane Paste Prawns (*Chao Tom*)   26
Prawn Spring Rolls (*Cha Tom*)   26

Vegetables & Salads
Cabbage Salad with Shredded Chicken
   (*Goi Ga Bap Cai*)   28
Fresh Salad Rolls (*Goi Cuon*)   28

Green Mango Salad (*Goi Xoai*)   30
Lotus Stem Salad (*Goi Ngo Sen*)   30

Pomelo Salad (*Goi Buoi*)   32
Squid Salad (*Goi Muc*)   32

Stir-fried Cockles with Bean Sprouts and
   Chinese Chives (*So Huyet Xao Gia He*)   34
Stir-fried Water Convolvulus with Fermented
   Bean Curd (*Rau Muong Xao Chao*)   34

Stir-fried Beef with Chinese Kale
   (*Cai Lan Xao Thit Bo*)   36
Stir-fried Squid with Baby Corn
   (*Muc Xao Bap Non*)   36

Banana Bud and Clam Salad
   (*Goi Bap Chuoi Ngheu*)   38

Meats
Chicken Curry (*Ca Ri Ga*)   38

Sautéed Chicken with Lemon Grass and
   Chilli (*Ga Xao Sa Ot*)   40
Grilled Chicken Breast with Kaffir Lime
   Leaves (*Ga Nuong La Chanh*)   40

Stewed Chicken with Green Peas
   (*Ga Nau Dau*)   42
Claypot Pepper Pork (*Thit Kho Tieu*)   42

Pork and Egg Stew with Coconut Juice
   (*Thit Kho Nuoc Dua*)   44
Salted Fried Pork Ribs (*Suon Muoi Chien*)   44

Grilled Meat Balls on Skewers (*Nem Nuong*)   46
Steamed Egg with Minced Pork
  (*Cha Trung Hap*)   46

Spiced Beef Stew (*Bo Kho-Banh Mi*)   48
Grilled Beef in Pointed Pepper Leaves
  (*Bo Nuong La Lot*)   48

Beef in Vinegar Hot Pot (*Bo Nhung Dam*)   50
Sautéed Frog Legs with Lemon Grass
  (*Ech Xao Sa Ot*)   50

Seafood
Simmered River Prawns (*Tom Cang Rim*)   52
Snails Stuffed with Minced Pork
  (*Oc Buou Nhoi Thit*)   52

Crispy Soft Shell Crabs (*Cua Lot Chien Gion*)   54
Crabs with Tamarind Sauce (*Cua Rang Me*)   54

Fish Steamed with Soy Beans
  (*Ca Chung Tuong*)   56
Fried Fish with Lemon Grass and Chilli
  (*Ca Chien Sa Ot*)   56

Simmered Fish (*Ca Kho To*)   58
Prawns and Pork Simmered in Coconut Juice
  (*Tep Rang Nuoc Dua*)   58

Steamed Prawns in Coconut Juice
  (*Tom Hap Nuoc Dua*)   60
Steamed Crabs in Beer Broth (*Cua Hap Bia*)   60

Stuffed Squid (*Muc Nhoi Thit*)   62
Steamed Squid with Ginger and Spring
  Onion (*Muc Hap Hanh Gung*)   62

Thang Long Fish Cake (*Cha Ca Thang Long*)   64
Crabs in Garlic and Pepper Salt
  (*Cua Rang Muoi*)   64

Deep-fried Prawns Coated with Sesame
  Seeds (*Tom Lan Me*)   66
Fried Mackerel with Fish Sauce
  (*Ca Thu Chien Sot Ca*)   66

Crispy Squid (*Muc Chien Gion*)   68

Rice
Rice Wrapped in Lotus Leaf
  (*Com Hoang Bao*)   68

Chicken Porridge (*Chao Ga*)   70
Vietnamese Fried Rice (*Com Chien*)   70

Desserts
Vietnamese Bo Bo Cha Cha (*Che Thung*)   72
Caramel Custard (*Banh Flan*)   72

Lotus Seeds with Agar-agar (*Che Sen Thach*)   74
Green Bean Paste with Coconut Milk
  (*Che Dau Xanh Danh*)   74

Glutinous Rice Balls (*Che Troi Nuoc*)   76
Banana Sago (*Che Chuoi Chung*)   76

Basic Recipes   **78**
Glossary   **80**
Weights & Measures   **84**

PREFACE

I was born in Thai Binh, a province located in the north of Vietnam. Thai Binh has a coastline stretching over 50 km, and it is characterised by many estuaries, seaports and beaches. With this proximity to the sea, there is an abundance of seafood. The north was also controlled by the Chinese for over 1,000 years, from 111 BC to AD 939, and thus, the food and cooking styles of the north are very similar to Chinese food. This includes stir-fries and soups, and a generally less spicy cuisine than that found in other parts of the country.

When I was young, I watched and helped my mother in the kitchen. That was the start of my culinary training in northern Vietnamese cuisine. I would help her cook our daily meals as well as whenever we had large gatherings of family and friends.

I then moved to Ho Chi Minh City (Saigon) where I began to discover the cuisine of the south. There, I enrolled myself in a cooking academy to train as a chef in Vietnamese cooking. I learnt more about the different cuisines of the central and south of Vietnam, as well as that of the north where I was born. During this time, I also travelled a lot throughout Vietnam, and I had the opportunity to taste and experience for myself the different cuisines.

Down towards the south and southeast, Vietnam shares a border with Laos, Thailand and Cambodia. The ingredients that these countries favour have gradually been incorporated into Vietnamese cooking, such as spices, curry, fish sauce, prawn paste, lemon grass, mint and basil, although the flavours are recognisably milder. Vietnam was also colonised by the French for about 100 years, and the impact on the cuisine was a preference for baguettes and paté.

The 70 recipes in this book include a variety of dishes from all over Vietnam. There is Thang Long fish cake from the north, sugar cane paste prawns and Hue-styled spicy beef and pork noodles from central Vietnam, and tamarind fish soup and Saigon pancake from the south.

Some of these recipes are simple home fare eaten for daily meals, such as pork cabbage roll soup and fried fish with lemon grass and chilli, while others are more festive fare, prepared for special gatherings of family and friends, such as net spring rolls and steamed prawns in coconut juice. There are also recipes that require more preparation time, such as grilled pork with vermicelli and the popular beef noodle soup, which are suitable for weekend meals.

It is my hope that you will be able to use these recipes to prepare authentic Vietnamese dishes and in the process, learn to appreciate the wonderful variety of food enjoyed throughout Vietnam.

Ha Mai

PORK CABBAGE ROLL SOUP
(CANH BAP CAI CUON THIT)
Cooking time: 30 min   Serves 4

INGREDIENTS
Minced pork	300 g
Shallots	3, peeled and finely chopped
Dried fine rice vermicelli (*beehoon*)	50 g, soaked in warm water for 5 minutes and chopped
Wood ear fungus	2–3, soaked to soften and chopped
Salt	
Ground white pepper	
White cabbage	500 g, leaves separated and blanched
Spring onions (scallions)	10, green part only, blanched
Water or stock	1 litre
Chicken seasoning powder	1 Tbsp
Fish sauce	1 Tbsp

GARNISH
Spring onion (scallion)	2 tsp, chopped
Coriander (cilantro)	1 tsp, finely chopped

METHOD
- Combine minced pork, shallots, rice vermicelli and wood ear fungus, then season to taste with salt and pepper.
- Put 1 Tbsp of minced pork mixture onto each cabbage leaf and roll up neatly. Secure with a length of spring onion.
- Bring water or stock to the boil and cook cabbage rolls for 5 minutes. Add salt, pepper, chicken seasoning powder and fish sauce.
- Ladle soup and cabbage rolls into individual serving bowls and sprinkle with chopped spring onion and coriander. Serve hot.

Tip:
- You also can use minced prawns (shrimps) in place of minced pork in this recipe.

MINCED BEEF AND TOMATO SOUP
(CANH BO RAU RAM)
Cooking time: 30 min   Serves 4

INGREDIENTS
Minced beef	200 g
Salt	
Ground white pepper	
Water or stock	1 litre
Tomatoes	2, cut into wedges
Onion	1, peeled and cut into wedges
Chicken seasoning powder	

GARNISH
Polygonum (*laksa*) leaves (*daun kesum*)	2 sprigs, finely chopped

METHOD
- Marinate beef with salt and pepper to taste.
- Bring water or stock to the boil. Add tomatoes, minced beef and onion. Bring to the boil again and season soup to taste with salt and chicken seasoning powder.
- Ladle soup into individual serving bowls and sprinkle with pepper and polygonum leaves. Serve hot with steamed rice.

From top: Pork Cabbage Roll Soup; Minced Beef and Tomato Soup

TAMARIND FISH SOUP (CANH CHUA CA)

Cooking time: 30 min   Serves 4

INGREDIENTS

Cooking oil	1 Tbsp
Garlic	4 cloves, peeled and chopped
Snakehead	1, about 400 g, cleaned and sliced
Stock	1 litre
Ladies' fingers (okra)	4, sliced
Tomatoes	2, cut into wedges
Pineapple	300 g, peeled and sliced
Yam	75 g, peeled and sliced
Bean sprouts	25 g
Tamarind (*asam*) pulp	50 g
Fish sauce	3 Tbsp
Sugar	1 Tbsp
Salt	
Ground white pepper	

GARNISH

Thai parsley	2 leaves, chopped
Red chilli	1, sliced

METHOD

- In a wok, heat oil and stir-fry garlic until fragrant. Remove garlic and set aside for garnish.
- Using the same oil, cook fish slices for 5 minutes.
- Pour in stock and bring to the boil until fish is cooked.
- Add ladies' fingers, tomatoes, pineapple, yam and bean sprouts. Reduce heat and simmer for a few minutes.
- Add tamarind pulp and fish sauce, sugar and salt to taste.
- Ladle soup into a large bowl. Sprinkle with pepper and garnish with parsley, sliced chilli and fried garlic. Serve hot with steamed rice.

Tip:

- *If snakehead is unavailable, any firm-fleshed fish is a good substitute. You can also use prawns (shrimps) if preferred.*

TOMATO AND EGG SOUP (CANH CA CHUA TRUNG)

Cooking time: 20 min   Serves 4

INGREDIENTS

Minced pork	200 g
Salt	
Ground white pepper	
Water or stock	1 litre
Tomatoes	3, cut into wedges
Eggs	2, beaten
Fish sauce	1 Tbsp
Sugar	1 tsp
Chicken seasoning powder	1 tsp

GARNISH

Spring onion (scallion)	1, chopped

METHOD

- Marinate minced pork with salt and pepper to taste.
- Bring water or stock to the boil then scoop minced pork in teaspoon by teaspoon so it does not clump together.
- Add tomatoes.
- Pour eggs in through a sieve and stir to get egg ribbons.
- Stir in fish sauce, sugar, chicken seasoning powder and $1/2$ tsp pepper.
- Garnish with spring onion and serve hot with steamed rice.

From top: Tamarind Fish Soup; Tomato and Egg Soup

PIG'S TROTTERS NOODLE SOUP (BANH CANH GIO HEO)

Cooking time: 2 hr   Serves 4–6

INGREDIENTS

Pig's trotters	1.2 kg, cleaned and cut into pieces
Salt	
Shallots	4, peeled and thinly sliced
Pork	200 g
Sugar	1/2 tsp
Chicken seasoning powder	1 tsp
Cooking oil	2 Tbsp
Short round rice noodles (*bee tai mak*)	500 g
Spring onions (scallions)	2–3, finely chopped
Coriander (cilantro)	2–3 sprigs, finely chopped
Ground white pepper	
Fish sauce	
Limes	2, cut into wedges
Red chilli	1, chopped

METHOD

- Soak pig's trotters in lightly salted water for 10 minutes. Wash and drain.
- Bring 3 litres water to the boil in a large pot. Add 1/2 tsp salt, a few slices of shallots and pig's trotters. Lower heat and simmer, skimming frequently to remove any scum that surfaces.
- When pig's trotters are half-cooked, add pork. When pork is cooked, remove and drain. Cool before slicing thinly.
- Add sugar, 1/2 tsp salt and chicken seasoning powder to stock.
- Heat oil and fry remaining sliced shallots until crisp. Drain well.
- Divide noodles equally into large serving bowls. Top with pork, pig's trotters, spring onions, fried shallots, coriander and pepper.
- Pour stock over and serve with fish sauce, lime wedges and chopped chilli on the side.

Tip:
- *Leave pot uncovered when simmering stock. This will help keep the stock clear.*

FISH TOMATO SOUP (CANH CA NAU NGOT)

Cooking time: 30 min   Serves 4

INGREDIENTS

Water or stock	1 litre
Freshwater fish fillets	500 g, cleaned and cut into large chunks
Tomatoes	2, cut into wedges
Red chilli	1, sliced
Lime juice	1 tsp
Fish sauce	1 Tbsp
Sugar	1 tsp
Chicken seasoning powder	1 tsp

GARNISH

Spring onions (scallions)	2–3, cut into 3-cm lengths
Chinese celery	2 sprigs, cut into 3-cm lengths

METHOD

- Bring water or stock to the boil and add fish.
- Bring to the boil again and add tomatoes, chilli, lime juice, fish sauce, sugar and chicken seasoning powder.
- Garnish with spring onions and Chinese celery. Serve hot with steamed rice or rice vermicelli (*beehoon*).

From top: Pig's Trotters Noodle Soup; Fish Tomato Soup

BITTER GOURD STUFFED WITH MINCED PORK SOUP (CANH KHO QUA NHOI THIT)

Cooking time: 1 hr   Serves 2–4

INGREDIENTS

Water	3 litres
Pork bones	500 g
Salt	
Bitter gourds	4, small, soaked in hot water to soften slightly
Minced pork	200 g
Ground white pepper	1/4 tsp
Spring onions (scallions)	4, white bulbous ends finely chopped and green parts blanched
Dried fine rice vermicelli (*beehoon*)	12 g, soaked in warm water for 10 minutes, then cut into 2-cm lengths
Wood ear fungus	3, soaked to soften then thinly sliced
Fish sauce	
Red chilli	1, chopped

GARNISH

Spring onion (scallion)	1, chopped
Coriander (cilantro)	1 sprig, finely chopped

METHOD

- Bring water to the boil and add pork bones and salt to taste. Simmer for 1 hour, skimming surface to remove any scum.
- Meanwhile, carefully cut a slit along the length of bitter gourds and remove seeds. Set aside.
- Combine minced pork with 1/4 tsp salt, pepper, chopped white bulbous ends of spring onions, rice vermicelli and wood ear fungus. Stuff mixture into bitter gourds.
- Tie blanched lengths of spring onions around bitter gourds.
- Place bitter gourds into stock and leave to boil until softened.
- Season stock with 1 Tbsp fish sauce and more salt if necessary.
- Garnish with spring onion and coriander. Sprinkle with pepper and serve with fish sauce and chilli on the side.

CHICKEN GLASS NOODLE SOUP (MIEN GA)

Cooking time: 2 hr   Serves 4–6

INGREDIENTS

Cooking oil	2 Tbsp
Shallots	3, peeled and finely chopped
Garlic	1 tsp, finely chopped
Chicken gizzard	100 g, thinly sliced
Wood ear fungus	10, soaked to soften then thinly sliced
Fish sauce	2 Tbsp
Sugar	1 tsp
Chicken seasoning powder	1 tsp
Water	3 litres
Salt	1 tsp
Whole chicken	1, about 1.2 kg, cleaned
Glass noodles (*tunghoon*)	200 g, soaked to soften then cut into shorter lengths
Ground white pepper	1/4 tsp
Red chilli	1, chopped
Limes	2, cut into wedges

GARNISH

Spring onions (scallions)	2–3, chopped
Coriander (cilantro)	2–3 sprigs, chopped
Polygonum (*laksa*) leaves (*daun kesum*)	1–2 sprigs, finely chopped

METHOD

- Heat cooking oil and fry shallots and garlic until fragrant.
- Add chicken gizzard and stir-fry for 5 minutes before adding wood ear fungus, fish sauce, sugar and chicken seasoning powder. Mix well. Set aside.
- In a large pot, bring water to the boil then add salt and chicken. Leave to boil for 30 minutes.
- Add stir-fried chicken gizzard and wood ear fungus. Season with more fish sauce, sugar and chicken seasoning powder to taste.
- When chicken is cooked, remove and leave to cool before shredding meat.
- Divide glass noodles equally into serving bowls. Top with shredded chicken meat, chicken gizzard and wood ear fungus.
- Pour stock over and garnish with spring onions, coriander and polygonum leaves. Sprinkle with some pepper and serve with chilli and lime wedges on the side.

From top: Bitter Gourd Stuffed with Minced Pork Soup; Chicken Glass Noodle Soup

CRAB NOODLE SOUP (BUN RIEU)

Cooking time: 2 hr   Serves 6

INGREDIENTS

Mud crabs	1 kg
Pork bones	1 kg
Dried prawns (shrimps)	50 g
Salt	
Cooking oil	1 Tbsp
Garlic	3 cloves, peeled and crushed
Tomatoes	2, large, each cut into wedges
Annatto seed oil (see pg 78)	1 Tbsp
Firm bean curd	2 pieces, cut into small cubes and fried
Tamarind (*asam*) pulp	1 Tbsp
Sugar	1 tsp
Fish sauce	2 Tbsp
Fine prawn (shrimp) paste	1 Tbsp
Fresh rice vermicelli (*beehoon*)	1 kg, blanched

GARNISH

Spring onion (scallion)	1, chopped
Coriander (cilantro)	1 sprig
Banana bud	1, outer layers removed, yellow centre shredded
Red chilli	1, thinly sliced
Bean sprouts	50 g
Mint leaves	2–3 sprigs
Thai parsley	2–3 leaves
Limes	2, large, cut into wedges
Fermented anchovy paste	

METHOD

- Pound crabs with some salt then mix with 2 litres water. Strain to get liquid then stir residue into another 2 litres water. Strain once more and discard residue.
- Pour strained water into a large pot. Add pork bones and dried prawns. Bring to the boil and add salt to taste. Leave to boil for 1 hour 30 minutes then strain stock.
- Heat oil in a pan and stir-fry garlic and tomatoes. Combine with annatto seed oil and pour into stock.
- Add fried bean curd and tamarind pulp. Season with sugar, fish sauce, prawn paste and salt.
- Divide rice vermicelli equally into 6 serving bowls. Pour stock over and garnish with spring onion. Serve remaining garnishes on the side.

CHICKEN NOODLE SOUP (PHO GA)

Cooking time: 2 hr   Serves 6

INGREDIENTS

Whole chicken	1, about 2 kg, cleaned
Chicken carcasses	1 kg, cleaned
Water	6 litres
Cinnamon stick	1, about 5 cm
Star anise	3
Ginger	5-cm knob, grilled until skin is burnt
Onions	3, large, grilled until skin is burnt
Salt	2 tsp
Sugar	2 tsp
Fish sauce	1 Tbsp
Fresh rice vermicelli (*beehoon*)	500 g, blanched
Bean sprouts	100 g, blanched
Ground white pepper	

GARNISH

Spring onions (scallions)	3, cut into 5-cm lengths
Coriander (cilantro)	1 sprig, chopped
Thai basil leaves	1 sprig
Thai parsley	2–3 leaves
Bean sprouts	50 g
Red chillies	4, sliced
Limes	3, large, cut into wedges
Chilli sauce	2 Tbsp
Fish sauce	2 Tbsp

METHOD

- Place chicken and carcasses in a large pot. Add water and bring to the boil over medium heat. Add cinnamon stick, star anise and grilled ginger and onions.
- When chicken is cooked, remove and place in cold water until cooled. Shred meat and set aside. Place carcass back into stock and continue to boil for 1 hour more.
- Remove and discard chicken carcasses. Add salt, sugar and fish sauce.
- Divide rice vermicelli and bean sprouts into 6 serving bowls. Top with shredded chicken.
- Pour hot stock over and sprinkle with pepper. Serve with garnish.

Tip:

- *If fresh rice vermicelli is unavailable, use 500 g dried rice sticks or vermicelli. Soak in cold water for 20 minutes then place into boiling water and cook for 5 minutes. Rinse under cold water and drain before using.*

From left: Crab Noodle Soup with Garnishes; Chilli Sauce; Chicken Noodle Soup with Garnishes

GRILLED PORK WITH VERMICELLI (BUN THIT NUONG)

Cooking time: 1 hr   Serves 6

INGREDIENTS

Pork shoulder or loin	600 g, sliced thinly
Dried rice vermicelli (*beehoon*)	1 kg
Peanuts (groundnuts)	100 g, roasted and crushed
Mixed fish sauce (see pg 78)	

MARINADE

Lemon grass (*serai*)	2 stalks, bulbous portions only, finely chopped
Garlic	1 tsp, finely chopped
Ground white pepper	1/4 tsp
Sugar	1 tsp
Fish sauce	1 Tbsp
Chicken seasoning powder	1 tsp
Red chilli	1, finely chopped

GARNISH

Pickled carrot and radish (see pg 79)	1 Tbsp
Thai basil leaves	2–3 sprigs
Bean sprouts	100 g
Lettuce	75 g, julienned
Cucumber	1, julienned

METHOD

- Combine marinade ingredients and marinate pork for 5 minutes.
- Soak rice vermicelli in cold water for 20 minutes then place into boiling water and cook for 5 minutes. Rinse under cold water, drain and set aside.
- Grill pork over a medium charcoal flame until golden brown.
- To serve, divide garnish equally into 6 serving bowls. Top with rice vermicelli and grilled pork. Sprinkle with peanuts and mixed fish sauce. Toss well before eating.

Tip:

- *You can also use grilled chicken or beef stir-fried with chopped lemon grass in place of pork.*

HANOI CHICKEN VERMICELLI (BUN THANG)

Cooking time: 2 hr   Serves 6

INGREDIENTS

Whole chicken	1, about 1.2 kg, cleaned
Water	4 litres
Shallots	5, peeled and sliced
Salt	1 tsp
Dried prawns (shrimps)	200 g
Chicken carcass	500 g, cleaned
Fish sauce	2 Tbsp
Chicken seasoning powder	1 tsp
Fine prawn (shrimp) paste	2 Tbsp
Dried rice vermicelli (*beehoon*)	400 g
Eggs	3, beaten, fried and thinly sliced
Ham	200 g, thinly sliced
Spring onions (scallions)	2, chopped

GARNISH

Red chillies	2, pounded
Fine prawn (shrimp) paste	
Bean sprouts	100 g
Lettuce	75 g, sliced
Mint leaves	12 g
Polygonum (*laksa*) leaves (*daun kesum*)	2–3 sprigs
Limes	2, cut into wedges

METHOD

- Place chicken into a large pot with water. Bring to the boil with shallots and salt for about 1 hour or until chicken is cooked. Remove chicken and leave to cool. Shred meat and set aside.
- Add dried prawns and chicken carcass and boil for another 20 minutes. Remove and discard chicken carcass and dried prawns. Stir in fish sauce, chicken seasoning powder and prawn paste.
- Soak rice vermicelli in cold water for 20 minutes then place into boiling water and cook for 5 minutes. Rinse under cold water and drain.
- Divide rice vermicelli equally into 6 serving bowls. Top with eggs, shredded chicken, ham and spring onion. Pour boiling stock over.
- Serve with garnish on the side.

From left: Grilled Pork with Vermicelli; Hanoi Chicken Vermicelli

19

HUE-STYLED SPICY BEEF AND PORK NOODLES (BUN BO HUE)

Cooking time: 4 hr   Serves 6

INGREDIENTS

Water	6 litres
Pork bones	2 kg, cleaned
Pork knuckles or leg	500 g, cleaned and deboned
Beef shin	500 g
Lemon grass (*serai*)	2 stalks, 1 bruised and 1 finely chopped
Fine prawn (shrimp) paste	1 Tbsp
Fish sauce	1 Tbsp
Salt	2 tsp
Sugar	2 tsp
Annatto seed oil (see pg 78)	2 Tbsp
Chilli powder	1/2 tsp
Thai parsley	2 leaves, finely cut
Dried rice vermicelli (*beehoon*)	500 g
Spring onions (scallions)	3, white part only, cut into 3-cm lengths
Onion	1, large, peeled and thinly sliced

GARNISH

Bean sprouts	50 g
Limes	2, large, cut into wedges
Red chillies	4, 2 finely sliced, 2 pounded
Fish sauce	

METHOD

- Bring water to the boil and add pork bones, pork, beef and bruised lemon grass. As stock boils, periodically reduce heat to medium and skim off any scum from surface.
- Simmer until meats are tender. Remove pork and soak in a bowl of hot water for 10 minutes until cool. Rinse and slice.
- Remove and discard pork bones and lemon grass. Remove beef and slice.
- Stir prawn paste, fish sauce, salt and sugar into stock and continue to simmer.
- Heat annatto seed oil and add chopped lemon grass and chilli powder. Stir-fry for a few minutes then add Thai parsley. Add to stock.
- Blanch vermicelli and spring onions. Divide equally into 6 serving bowls. Top with pork, beef spring onion and onion. Pour hot stock over.
- Serve with bean sprouts, lime wedges and sliced chillies. Mix pounded chillies into fish sauce and serve on the side.

BEEF NOODLE SOUP (PHO BO)

Cooking time: 4 hr   Serves 6

INGREDIENTS

Water	3 litres
Beef marrow	2 kg
Beef brisket	500 g
Salt	
Ginger	5-cm knob, grilled until skin is burnt
Onions	3, large, grilled until skin is burnt
Shallots	3, grilled until skin is burnt
Star anise	3
Cinnamon sticks	2, each about 5 cm
Ground white pepper	
Fresh flat rice noodles (*hor fun*)	600 g, blanched
Bean sprouts	100 g, blanched
Sirloin or flank steak	200 g, thinly sliced and refrigerated

GARNISH

Onion	1, large, peeled and sliced
Spring onions (scallions)	2–3, finely sliced
Coriander (cilantro)	3 sprigs, chopped
Red chillies	4, chopped
Hoisin sauce	3 Tbsp
Chili sauce	2 Tbsp
Limes	2, large, cut into wedges
Thai basil leaves	5 sprigs
Thai parsley	5 leaves, chopped
Bean sprouts	50 g
Mixed fish sauce (see pg 78)	

METHOD

- Bring water to the boil in a large pot. Add beef marrow and brisket. As stock boils, periodically reduce heat to medium and skim off any scum from surface.
- Add a pinch of salt, grilled ginger, onions and shallots, star anise and cinnamon. Boil for 30 minutes more then remove brisket and slice. Leave stock to simmer for another 3 hours.
- Remove and discard beef marrow. Add salt and pepper to taste.
- Divide rice vermicelli and bean sprouts equally into 6 serving bowls. Top with raw sirloin or flank beef.
- Pour stock over and sprinkle with pepper. Top with some garnish and serve the rest on the side.

From top: Hue-styled Spicy Beef and Pork Noodles; Beef Noodle Soup

NET SPRING ROLLS (CHA GIO RE)

Cooking time: 1 hr   Serves 4–6

INGREDIENTS

Cooking oil for deep-frying

NET WRAP

Rice flour	250 g
Tapioca flour	25 g
Egg	1
Sugar	1/2 tsp
Salt	1/4 tsp
Warm water	250 ml

STUFFING

Minced pork	200 g
Carrot	25 g, julienned
Yam	200 g, peeled and julienned
Prawns (shrimps)	200 g, peeled, deveined and minced
Crabmeat	100 g
Spring onion (scallion)	1, white portion only, finely chopped
Coriander (cilantro)	1 tsp, finely chopped
Garlic	1 tsp, chopped and fried
Shallot	1 tsp, chopped and fried
Ground white pepper	1 tsp
Chicken seasoning powder	1 tsp
Salt	1/4 tsp
Sugar	1 tsp
Egg	1
Wood ear fungus	3, soaked to soften, thinly sliced

GARNISH

Lettuce, mint, Thai basil and sliced cucumber
Mixed fish sauce (see pg 78)

METHOD

- Combine net wrap ingredients and leave for 2–3 hours. Combine stuffing ingredients and set aside.
- Heat a non-stick pan over medium heat. Dip fingers of one hand into net wrap batter. Bring it up and wait for a few seconds for batter to run down in long strips. Place a plate under your hand to catch any drip. Form a round lacy net in hot pan. Allow for a few seconds for net wrap to cook before removing to a plate. Make 40 pieces of net wrap.
- Lay a net wrap on a plate and scoop 1 heaped Tbsp of filling onto the centre. Fold left and right hand sides of net wrap in towards centre to enclose filling then roll up from the edge closest to you to form a neat roll. Make 40 rolls.
- Heat oil over medium heat then fry spring rolls in batches until golden brown. Remove and drain well.
- Serve with garnish and mixed fish sauce on the side.

GOLDEN SPRING ROLLS (CHA GIO)

Cooking time: 30 min   Serves 4–6

INGREDIENTS

Vietnamese rice paper	30 sheets, sprinkled with water to soften
Cooking oil for deep-frying	

FILLING

Minced pork	200 g
Crabmeat	50 g
Prawns (shrimps)	100 g, peeled, deveined and minced
Yam	100 g, peeled and julienned
Carrot	25 g, julienned
Turnip	75 g, peeled and julienned
Wood ear fungus	3, soaked to soften, thinly sliced
Glass noodles (*tunghoon*)	25 g, soaked to soften then cut into 0.3-cm lengths
Shallots	2, peeled and finely chopped
Garlic	1 tsp, finely chopped
Egg	1, well beaten
Ground white pepper	1 tsp
Salt	1/2 tsp
Sugar	1 tsp

GARNISH

Lettuce, mint, Thai basil and sliced cucumber
Mixed fish sauce (see pg 78)

METHOD

- In a large bowl, combine filling ingredients and mix well.
- Place a sheet of rice paper on a plate and scoop 1 heaped Tbsp of filling onto the centre. Fold left and right hand sides of rice paper in towards the centre to enclose filling. Then roll up from the edge closest to you to form a neat roll. Make 30 rolls.
- Heat oil over medium heat and deep-fry rolls in batches until golden brown. Remove and drain well.
- Place a spring roll on a lettuce leaf and top with mint leaves, basil leaves and cucumber slices. Roll up and dip into mixed fish sauce before eating.

Tip:

- *When making the spring rolls, do not roll them up too tight or the rice paper might tear.*

From top: Net Spring Rolls; Golden Spring Rolls

CRISPY CHICKEN WINGS WITH FISH SAUCE (CANH GA CHIEN NUOC MAM)

Cooking time: 30 min   Serves 4

INGREDIENTS

Chicken wings	1 kg, about 6
Corn flour (cornstarch)	2 Tbsp
Cooking oil for deep-frying	

MARINADE

Garlic	1 bulb, peeled, finely chopped and squeezed for juice
Fish sauce	2 Tbsp
Chicken seasoning powder	1/2 tsp
Ground white pepper	1 tsp
Sugar	1/2 tsp

METHOD

- Cut each chicken wing at the mid joint.
- Combine marinade ingredients and marinate chicken for 1 hour.
- Drain chicken and coat well with corn flour.
- Heat oil over medium heat until it is very hot. Deep-fry chicken until golden brown.
- Remove and drain well. Serve hot.

Tip:

- *For this dish to be even more tasty, prepare a special dip. Mix 1 tsp salt, 1 tsp ground white pepper and 1 Tbsp lime juice. Dip chicken in before eating.*

SAIGON PANCAKE (BANH XEO)

Cooking time: 15 min   Serves 4

INGREDIENTS

Rice flour	200 g
Turmeric powder	1/2 tsp
Water	250 ml
Salt	
Coconut milk	150 ml
Spring onion (scallion)	1 Tbsp, finely chopped
Cooking oil	2 Tbsp
Lean pork	200 g, thinly sliced
Prawns (shrimps)	200 g, peeled and deveined
Onion	1, peeled and thinly sliced
Bean sprouts	100 g
Split green beans	200 g, soaked and steamed until soft
Vietnamese rice paper	10 sheets, sprinkled with water to soften

GARNISH

Mixed fish sauce (see pg 78)
Lettuce, mint, sliced cucumber and pickled carrot and radish (see pg 79)

METHOD

- In a large mixing bowl, blend rice flour and turmeric powder with water, then add a pinch of salt, coconut milk and spring onion. Mix well into a batter.
- In a large frying pan (skillet), heat cooking oil over medium heat until very hot. Add pork, prawns and onion and stir-fry for 2–3 minutes until meats are lightly cooked.
- Stir batter well and scoop a ladleful into pan. Add bean sprouts and green beans. Cover for 5 minutes until pancake is crisp. Fold pancake into half and continue to cook for another 5 minutes. Transfer to a plate.
- Serve pancake with mixed fish sauce for dipping and rice paper, lettuce, mint leaves, cucumber and pickled carrot and radish on the side.
- To assemble, place a sheet of rice paper on a plate and top with a small piece of pancake and some garnish. Wrap and dip into mixed fish sauce before eating.

Tip:

- *Use other meats such as chicken or squid as preferred.*

From left: Crispy Chicken Wings with Fish Sauce; Saigon Pancake with Garnishes and Mixed Fish Sauce

SUGARCANE PASTE PRAWNS (CHAO TOM)

Cooking time: 1 hr   Serves 4

INGREDIENTS

Prawns (shrimps)	500 g, peeled and deveined
Salt	1/2 tsp
Spring onions (scallions)	5, white portions only, chopped
Sugar	1 tsp
Ground white pepper	1/2 tsp
Chicken seasoning powder	1/2 tsp
Vegetable oil	2 Tbsp
Vietnamese rice paper	12 sheets, sprinkled with water to soften

GARNISH

Lettuce	100 g
Mint	25 g
Pickled carrot and radish (see pg 79)	150 g
Cucumber	1/2, julienned
Dried fine rice vermicelli (*beehoon*)	50 g, blanched
Mixed fish sauce (see pg 78)	250 ml
Sugarcane sticks	6, each 10-cm long, peeled

METHOD

- Mix prawns with a pinch of salt then rinse and dry thoroughly. Grind or pound prawns with spring onions, remaining salt, sugar, pepper and chicken seasoning powder.
- Oil your fingers to prevent prawn paste from sticking to them. Divide prawn paste equally into 6 portions. Using your fingers, mould one portion around a stick of sugar cane. Continue to make another 5 sticks.
- Steam for 10 minutes then grill over medium charcoal heat until lightly browned or deep-fry until golden brown.
- To assemble, lay a sheet of rice paper on a plate. Place a lettuce leaf, some mint leaves, pickled carrot and radish, cucumber and vermicelli on top. Remove cooked prawn paste from a sugarcane stick and place on top. Roll rice paper up and dip into mixed fish sauce before eating.

PRAWN SPRING ROLLS (CHA TOM)

Cooking time: 30 min   Serves 4

INGREDIENTS

Prawns (shrimps)	1 kg, peeled and deveined
Fresh coconut juice	from 1 young coconut
Spring onion (scallion)	1 Tbsp, white portion only, finely chopped
Ground white pepper	1/2 tsp
Salt	1 tsp
Sugar	1 tsp
Eggs	3, whites and yolks separated
Vietnamese rice paper	10 large sheets, sprinkled with water to soften
Tapioca flour or corn flour (cornstarch)	5 Tbsp
Cooking oil for deep-frying	

GARNISH

Mixed fish sauce (see pg 78), plum sauce or mayonnaise
Lettuce and sliced cucumber

METHOD

- Soak prawns in coconut juice for 10 minutes, then rinse and dry thoroughly. Discard juice.
- Grind or pound prawns together with spring onion, pepper, salt and sugar until mixture is smooth and sticky. Add 2 egg whites and mix well.
- Beat egg yolks and apply a thick layer onto each sheet of rice paper.
- Divide prawn mixture into 10 equal parts and spoon each part in long strips onto each sheet of rice paper. Roll up neatly into long spring rolls and cut each roll into 4 pieces (each about 5-cm long).
- Dip into remaining beaten egg yolks and roll in tapioca or corn flour until well-coated.
- Heat oil over medium heat and deep-fry rolls until golden brown. Remove and drain well.
- Serve with mixed fish sauce, plum sauce or mayonnaise for dipping and lettuce and cucumber on the side.

Anti-clockwise from top left: Sugarcane Paste Prawns; Sugarcane Paste Prawn Rolls; Prawn Spring Rolls

CABBAGE SALAD WITH SHREDDED CHICKEN
(GOI GA BAP CAI)

Preparation time: 20 min   Serves 4

INGREDIENTS

Chicken breast	200 g, cooked and shredded
Cabbage	200 g, finely sliced
Carrot	1, coarsely grated
Polygonum (*laksa*) leaves (*daun kesum*)	1 tsp, finely chopped
Salad dressing (see pg 79)	1 Tbsp
Prawn crackers	8, deep-fried

METHOD
- Combine chicken, cabbage, carrot and polygonum leaves in a large mixing bowl.
- Add salad dressing and toss well to combine.
- Arrange salad on a plate and serve with prawn crackers.

FRESH SALAD ROLLS
(GOI CUON)

Preparation time: 30 min   Makes 8 Rolls

INGREDIENTS

Dried fine rice vermicelli (*beehoon*)	25 g
Vietnamese rice paper	8 sheets, sprinkled with water to soften
Lettuce	100 g
Cucumber	1, thinly sliced
Carrot	1, thinly sliced
Mint leaves	2–3 sprigs
Thai basil leaves	2–3 sprigs
Bean sprouts	50 g
Chinese chives (*kucai*)	8, each cut into 2
Pork belly	100 g, cooked and sliced
Tiger prawns (shrimps)	200 g, deveined, cooked, peeled and sliced lengthwise in half
Peanut sauce (see pg 79)	

METHOD
- Soak rice vermicelli in cold water for 20 minutes then place into boiling water and cook for 5 minutes. Rinse under cold water, drain and set aside.
- Place a sheet of rice paper on a plate. Arrange lettuce, cucumber, carrot, mint leaves, basil leaves, bean sprouts, chives and vermicelli on the rice paper, along the edge closest to you. Top with slices of pork and prawns.
- Fold the edge of the rice paper closest to you over the filling. Then fold the left and right hand sides over and roll the spring roll away from you to form a neat parcel. Continue to make 7 more rolls.
- Serve with peanut sauce as a dip.

Anti-clockwise from top: Cabbage Salad with Shredded Chicken; Fresh Salad Rolls; Peanut Sauce

GREEN MANGO SALAD (GOI XOAI)

Preparation time: 20 min   Serves 4

INGREDIENTS

Green mangoes	300 g, peeled and julienned
Dried prawns (shrimps)	2 Tbsp, washed and soaked in warm water
Mint leaves	1 Tbsp, finely chopped
Salad dressing (see pg 79)	1 Tbsp
Mixed fish sauce (see pg 78)	
Prawn crackers	8, deep-fried

GARNISH

White sesame seeds	1 tsp, toasted

METHOD

- Combine mangoes, dried prawns and mint leaves in a bowl. Toss well with salad dressing.
- Arrange salad on a serving plate and garnish with sesame seeds.
- Serve with mixed fish sauce and prawn crackers on the side.

LOTUS STEM SALAD (GOI NGO SEN)

Preparation time: 20 min   Serves 4

INGREDIENTS

Salad dressing (see pg 79)	1 Tbsp
Mixed fish sauce (see pg 78)	
Prawn crackers	8, deep-fried

SALAD

Pickled carrot (see pg 79)	150 g
Lotus stems	200 g, washed and cut into 5-cm lengths
Prawns (shrimps)	150 g, deveined, cooked and peeled
Lean pork	100 g, cooked and thinly sliced
Onion	$1/2$, peeled and thinly sliced
Polygonum (*laksa*) leaves (*daun kesum*)	1 Tbsp, finely chopped

GARNISH

Crushed peanuts (groundnuts)	1 Tbsp
Fried shallots	1 tsp

METHOD

- In a large bowl, combine all salad ingredients and mix well. Add salad dressing and toss gently.
- Arrange salad on a serving plate. Garnish with ground peanuts and fried shallots.
- Serve immediately with mixed fish sauce and prawn crackers on the side.

Chef's Note:

- *Most Vietnamese salads like this one taste best if served immediately after it is prepared. Thus, try to prepare it just before serving.*

From top: Green Mango Salad; Lotus Stem Salad

POMELO SALAD
(GOI BUOI)

Preparation time: 20 min   Serves 4

INGREDIENTS

Salad dressing (see pg 79)	2 Tbsp
Prawn crackers	8, deep-fried

SALAD

Pomelo or grapefruit	1, peeled and segmented
Lean pork	50 g, cooked and thinly sliced
Prawns (shrimps)	100 g, deveined, cooked and peeled
Polygonum (*laksa*) leaves (*daun kesum*)	1 tsp, chopped

GARNISH

White sesame seeds	1 Tbsp, toasted

METHOD

- Peel membrane from pomelo or grapefruit segments and remove sacs.
- Combine sacs with pork, prawns and polygonum leaves in a large mixing bowl. Add salad dressing and toss well to combine.
- Transfer salad to a serving plate and garnish with sesame seeds. Serve with prawn crackers on the side.

SQUID SALAD
(GOI MUC)

Preparation time: 30 min   Serves 4

INGREDIENTS

Water	500 ml
Salt	
Rice vinegar	2 Tbsp
Salad dressing (see pg 79)	1 Tbsp
Prawn crackers	8, deep-fried

SALAD

Squid	400 g, cleaned
Ginger	2.5-cm knob, peeled and julienned
Onion	$1/2$, peeled and thinly sliced
Mint leaves	1 tsp, finely chopped

GARNISH

White sesame seeds	1 tsp, toasted
Red chilli	1, seeded and julienned

METHOD

- Cut squid crosswise into narrow sections.
- Fill a pot with water, add a little salt and rice vinegar and bring to the boil. Blanch squid quickly for 2 minutes then place in ice so squid stays crunchy.
- Combine salad ingredients with squid in a large bowl. Toss well with salad dressing.
- Serve with prawn crackers and garnish with sesame seeds and chilli.

From top: Pomelo Salad; Squid Salad

STIR-FRIED COCKLES WITH BEAN SPROUTS AND CHINESE CHIVES
(SO HUYET XAO GIA HE)

Cooking time: 30 min   Serves 4

INGREDIENTS

Cockles	1 kg, cleaned
Cooking oil	1 Tbsp
Garlic	1/2 Tbsp, finely chopped
Bean sprouts	100 g
Chinese chives (*kucai*)	40 g, cut into 5-cm lengths
Salt	1/4 tsp
Ground white pepper	1/4 tsp
Sugar	1/4 tsp
Fish sauce	1/4 tsp

METHOD

- Place cockles in boiling water for 5 minutes. Shell and set aside.
- Heat cooking oil and stir-fry garlic until fragrant. Add cockles and sauté for a few minutes.
- Add bean sprouts and Chinese chives and sauté.
- Season with salt, pepper, sugar and fish sauce to taste. Serve with steamed rice.

STIR-FRIED WATER CONVOLVULUS WITH FERMENTED BEAN CURD
(RAU MUONG XAO CHAO)

Cooking time: 15 min   Serves 4

INGREDIENTS

Water convolvulus (*kangkung*)	500 g
Red fermented bean curd	1 Tbsp
Sugar	1/2 tsp
Red chilli	1, finely chopped
Cooking oil	1 Tbsp
Garlic	1 clove, peeled and finely chopped

METHOD

- Wash water convolvulus and break into short lengths.
- In a small bowl, add fermented bean curd, sugar and chilli and mix well.
- Heat cooking oil and sauté garlic until fragrant. Add water convolvulus and sauté.
- Stir well for 5 minutes. Serve with steamed rice.

From top: Stir-fried Cockles with Bean Sprouts and Chinese Chives; Stir-fried Water Convolvulus with Fermented Bean Curd

STIR-FRIED BEEF WITH CHINESE KALE (CAI LAN XAO THIT BO)

Cooking time: 15 min   Serves 4

INGREDIENTS

Beef tenderloin	200 g, thinly sliced
Rice wine	1 tsp
Salt	
Corn flour (cornstarch)	$^1/_2$ tsp
Cooking oil	
Chinese kale (*kailan*)	500 g, cut into 5-cm lengths
Garlic	1 Tbsp, finely chopped
Sugar	$^1/_4$ tsp
Fish sauce	1 tsp

METHOD

- Marinate beef with rice wine, $^1/_4$ tsp salt and corn flour. Leave for 10 minutes.
- Bring a pot of water to the boil then add some salt and cooking oil. Blanch Chinese kale and drain.
- Heat a wok with 1 Tbsp cooking oil and stir-fry garlic until fragrant.
- Add beef and stir-fry for 5 minutes. Season with sugar, fish sauce and salt to taste.
- Add Chinese kale and mix well. Serve with steamed rice.

Tip:
- *Besides Chinese kale, you can also use other types of vegetables in this recipe.*

STIR–FRIED SQUID WITH BABY CORN (MUC XAO BAP NON)

Cooking time: 20 min   Serves 4

INGREDIENTS

Squid	500 g, cleaned
Rice wine	1 Tbsp
Cooking oil	1 Tbsp
Garlic	1 tsp, finely chopped
Onion	1, peeled and cut in wedges
Carrot	$^1/_2$, sliced and blanched
Snow peas	25 g, blanched
Baby corn	150 g, blanched
Salt	$^1/_4$ tsp
Sugar	$^1/_4$ tsp
Fish sauce	1 tsp
Ground white pepper	1 dash

GARNISH
Coriander (cilantro)

DIPPING SAUCE

Fish sauce	2 Tbsp
Red chilli	1, sliced

METHOD

- Slit open squid tubes and flatten. Make diagonal cuts on the inner surface then slice.
- Boil some water in a pot and add rice wine. Blanch squid then drain.
- Heat oil and stir-fry garlic until fragrant. Add onion then carrot, snow peas, baby corn and drained squid.
- Add salt, sugar and fish sauce then stir-fry for another 5 minutes. Remove from heat and transfer to plate.
- Sprinkle with pepper and garnish with coriander.
- Combine dipping sauce ingredients. Serve together with squid and steamed rice.

Tip:
- *As a variation to this recipe, replace squid with prawns (shrimps).*

From top: Stir-fried Beef with Chinese Kale; Stir-fried Squid with Baby Corn

BANANA BUD AND CLAM SALAD
(GOI BAP CHUOI NGHEU)
Cooking time: 20 min   Serves 4

INGREDIENTS
Salad dressing (see pg 79)	1 Tbsp
Prawn crackers	8, deep-fried

SALAD
Banana bud	1, outer layers removed, yellow centre shredded
Lime juice	3 Tbsp
Salt	1/8 tsp
Clams	1 kg
Mint leaves	1 Tbsp, finely chopped
Lean pork	100 g, cooked and thinly sliced
Sesame seeds	1 Tbsp, toasted
Fried shallots	1 tsp

METHOD
- Soak shredded banana bud in a bowl of water with lime juice and salt for 30 minutes then drain. This will make it whiter in colour.
- Bring a pot of water to the boil and cook clams. Shell and set aside.
- Combine all salad ingredients and toss well with salad dressing. Serve with prawn crackers on the side.

Tip:
- *If you do not take clams, replace with shredded chicken.*

CHICKEN CURRY
(CA RI GA)
Cooking time: 30 min   Serves 4

INGREDIENTS
Whole chicken	1, about 1.2 kg, cleaned, skinned and chopped into large pieces
Salt	
Sugar	
Curry powder	2 Tbsp
Red chilli	1, finely chopped
Cooking oil	1 Tbsp
Garlic	1 tsp, finely chopped
Lemon grass (*serai*)	2 stalks, bulbous portions only, bruised
Annatto seed oil (see pg 78)	1 Tbsp
Coconut milk	125 ml
Water	2.5 litres
Potatoes	300 g, peeled, cut into big cubes and deep-fried
Onion	1, peeled and cut into wedges
Sweet potatoes	200 g, peeled, cut into big cubes and deep-fried

METHOD
- Marinate chicken with 1/2 tsp salt, 1 tsp sugar, 1 Tbsp curry powder and chilli for 1 hour.
- Heat oil in a pot and stir-fry garlic and lemon grass until fragrant. Add remaining curry powder and annatto seed oil. Fry until curry is fragrant.
- Add chicken and continue to stir-fry for a few more minutes. Add half the coconut milk and water. Reduce heat and simmer.
- Add potatoes and simmer until chicken and potatoes are cooked. Add salt and sugar to taste if necessary. Add remaining coconut milk and stir.
- Remove and discard lemon grass. Serve with steamed rice, French baguette or noodles.

From top: Banana Bud and Clam Salad; Chicken Curry

SAUTÉED CHICKEN WITH LEMON GRASS AND CHILLI (GA XAO SA OT)

Cooking time: 1 hr   Serves 4

INGREDIENTS

Red chillies	2, seeded
Lemon grass (*serai*)	2 stalks, bulbous portions only, thinly sliced
Garlic	5 cloves, peeled and chopped
Chicken pieces	500 g
Salt	1/2 tsp
Ground white pepper	1/4 tsp
Sugar	1 tsp
Annatto seed oil (see pg 78)	1 tsp
Chicken seasoning powder	1 tsp
Cooking oil	2 Tbsp

METHOD

- Pound or blend (process) chillies, lemon grass and garlic together until fine.
- Marinate chicken with one-third of pounded mixture, salt, pepper, sugar, annatto seed oil and chicken seasoning powder for 30 minutes.
- Heat oil in a wok and stir-fry remaining pounded mixture until fragrant and golden brown.
- Add chicken and stir-fry for 10 minutes until chicken is cooked.
- Stir in 125 ml water and simmer for a further 10 minutes until chicken is tender. Serve with steamed rice.

GRILLED CHICKEN BREAST WITH KAFFIR LIME LEAVES (GA NUONG LA CHANH)

Cooking time: 30 min   Serves 4–6

INGREDIENTS

Chicken breast	1 kg, deboned
Garlic juice	1 Tbsp
Spring onion (scallion)	1 Tbsp, white portion only, finely chopped
Salt	1/2 tsp
Ground white pepper	1/2 tsp
Chicken seasoning powder	1 tsp
Sugar	1/2 Tbsp
Rice wine	1 Tbsp
Annatto seed oil (see pg 78)	1 Tbsp
Kaffir lime leaves	20
Toothpicks	20

DIP

Limes	2, halved
Salt	2 tsp
Ground white pepper	2 tsp

METHOD

- Cut chicken breast into 20 large cubes. Marinade with garlic juice, spring onion, salt, pepper, chicken seasoning powder, sugar, rice wine and annatto seed oil for 20 minutes.
- Wrap each chicken breast cube in a kaffir lime leaf and use a toothpick to secure.
- Place in an oven and cook at 250°C for 15 minutes or until chicken turns golden brown. Arrange on a plate.
- Prepare dip. Squeeze juice from limes then mix with salt and pepper. Serve with grilled chicken.

From top: Sautéed Chicken with Lemon Grass and Chilli; Grilled Chicken Breast with Kaffir Lime Leaves

STEWED CHICKEN WITH GREEN PEAS (GA NAU DAU)

Cooking time: 1 hr   Serves 4

INGREDIENTS

Whole chicken	1, about 1.2 kg, cleaned
Caramel syrup (see pg 78)	1 Tbsp
Cooking oil for deep-frying	
Ground white pepper	1 tsp
Salt	1 tsp
Onion	1, large, peeled and diced
Annatto seed oil (see pg 78)	2 Tbsp
Tomato paste	200 g
Tomato ketchup	2 Tbsp
Fresh coconut juice	from 2 young coconuts
Carrots	2, cut into large chunks
Green peas	50 g
Sugar	1 Tbsp
Chicken seasoning powder	2 Tbsp
Tapioca flour	2 Tbsp, mixed with 4 Tbsp water
Coriander (cilantro)	2–3 sprigs

METHOD

- Rub chicken with caramel syrup. Heat oil and deep-fry chicken until golden brown. Drain well then rinse chicken under running water. Chop into pieces and marinate with pepper and salt.
- Heat 2 Tbsp oil and stir-fry onion until fragrant. Add annatto seed oil, half the tomato paste and tomato ketchup. Cook for 5 minutes then add chicken. Mix well.
- Pour in coconut juice and enough water to cover chicken. Bring to the boil. Reduce heat and simmer until chicken is tender.
- Add carrots and green peas. Cook until carrots are soft. Add sugar and chicken seasoning powder. Adjust to taste with salt.
- Slowly stir in tapioca flour mixture until stew is thick.
- Serve sprinkled with pepper and coriander and French baguette on the side.

CLAYPOT PEPPER PORK (THIT KHO TIEU)

Cooking time: 30 min   Serves 4

INGREDIENTS

Lean pork	500 g, sliced
Fish sauce	3 Tbsp
Sugar	1 tsp
Caramel syrup (see pg 78)	1 tsp
Ground black pepper	
Red chilli	1, finely chopped
Spring onion (scallion)	1 tsp, white portion only, finely chopped
Salt	$1/4$ tsp
Cooking oil	1 tsp
Water or stock	125 ml

METHOD

- Marinade pork with fish sauce, sugar, caramel syrup, 1 tsp pepper, chilli, spring onion and salt for 1 hour.
- Heat oil in a claypot and sauté pork for 5 minutes.
- Add water or stock and bring to the boil. Lower heat and simmer until liquid evaporates and meat is cooked.
- Sprinkle some pepper over and serve with steamed rice.

From top: Stewed Chicken with Green Peas; Claypot Pepper Pork

PORK AND EGG STEW WITH COCONUT JUICE (THIT KHO NUOC DUA)

Cooking time: 1 hr   Serves 4

INGREDIENTS

Lean pork	1 kg, cut into big pieces
Spring onion (scallion)	1 Tbsp, white portion only, finely chopped
Garlic	1 tsp, finely chopped
Fish sauce	3 Tbsp
Sugar	1 Tbsp
Ground white pepper	1/4 tsp
Caramel syrup (see pg 78)	1/4 tsp
Cooking oil	1 Tbsp
Fresh coconut juice	from 1 young coconut
Eggs	5, hard-boiled and peeled

METHOD

- Marinade pork with spring onion, garlic, fish sauce, sugar, pepper and caramel syrup for 1 hour.
- Heat cooking oil in a pot and stir-fry pork for 5 minutes. Pour in coconut juice and simmer for 10 minutes then add eggs.
- Continue to cook for about 30 minutes more until meat is soft. Adjust to taste with salt and fish sauce. Serve with steamed rice.

Tips:
- *This dish can be prepared in advance and kept refrigerated for up to 1 week. Simply reheat before serving.*
- *If you prefer a more fatty cut of meat, use pork belly.*

SALTED FRIED PORK RIBS (SUON MUOI CHIEN)

Cooking time: 20 min   Serves 2–4

INGREDIENTS

Pork ribs	500 g, cut into small pieces
Salt	1/2 tsp
Ground white pepper	1/2 tsp
Chicken seasoning powder	1/2 tsp
Cooking oil for deep-frying	
Garlic	1 Tbsp, finely chopped

METHOD

- Marinate pork ribs with 1/4 tsp salt, 1/4 tsp pepper and chicken seasoning powder. Leave for 10 minutes.
- Heat oil in a wok and deep-fry pork ribs until golden brown. Remove, drain and set aside.
- In a clean wok, heat 1 Tbsp oil and stir-fry garlic until fragrant.
- Add pork ribs and season with remaining salt and pepper. Stir-fry for a few minutes to mix well. Serve hot with a salad on the side as desired.

From left: Pork and Egg Stew with Coconut Juice; Salted Fried Pork Ribs

GRILLED MEAT BALLS ON SKEWERS (NEM NUONG)

Cooking time: 1 hr   Serves 4

INGREDIENTS

Lean minced pork	400 g
Pork fat	100 g
Garlic	1 tsp, finely chopped
Spring onions (scallions)	5, white portions only
Sugar	1/2 Tbsp
Ground white pepper	1/2 tsp
Fish sauce	2 Tbsp, simmered until dry
Salt	1/2 tsp
Vietnamese rice paper	10 sheets, sprinkled with water to soften
Butter lettuce	1 head
Mint leaves	4–5 sprigs
Cucumber	1, peeled and thinly sliced
Pickled carrot and radish (see pg 79)	150 g
Dried fine rice vermicelli (*beehoon*)	25 g, soaked and steamed for 5 minutes
Chopped peanuts (groundnuts)	1 Tbsp
Bean paste dip (see pg 78) or mixed fish sauce (see pg 78)	
Bamboo skewers	10

METHOD
- Blend (process) minced pork and fat in a blender. Then use a mortar and pestle and pound mixture with garlic, spring onions, sugar, pepper, dried fish sauce and salt.
- Using your hands, form the mixture into 30 balls. Skewer 3 meat balls onto each bamboo skewer and cook over a charcoal grill.
- To assemble, lay a sheet of rice paper on a plate. Arrange butter lettuce, mint leaves, cucumber, pickled carrot and radish, rice vermicelli, peanuts and meat balls on top. Roll up and dip into bean paste dip or mixed fish sauce before eating.

STEAMED EGG WITH MINCED PORK (CHA TRUNG HAP)

Cooking time: 30 min   Serves 4

INGREDIENTS

Eggs	5
Minced pork	100 g
Wood ear fungus	3, soaked to soften and thinly sliced
Glass noodles (*tunghoon*)	25 g, soaked to soften, drained and cut into 1-cm lengths
Spring onion (scallion)	1 tsp each of white and green portions, finely chopped
Coriander (cilantro)	2–3 sprigs, finely chopped
Salt	1/4 tsp
Sugar	1 tsp
Ground white pepper	1/2 tsp

METHOD
- Reserve 2 egg yolks and beat remaining eggs.
- Mix all remaining ingredients into beaten eggs.
- Pour mixture into a large heatproof (flameproof) bowl and steam covered over medium heat for about 25 minutes.
- Beat reserved egg yolks and pour over steamed egg mixture. Steam for a further 5 minutes.
- Garnish as desired and serve hot with steamed rice.

Tip:
- *To test if the dish is cooked, simply insert a bamboo skewer into the thickest part. If the skewer comes out clean, the dish is cooked.*

Clockwise from top: Grilled Meat Balls on Skewers; Grilled Meat Ball Rolls with Bean Paste Dip; Steamed Egg with Minced Pork

SPICED BEEF STEW
(BO KHO-BANH MI)

Cooking time: 2 hr   Serves 4

INGREDIENTS

Beef shank	1 kg, cut into large cubes
Curry powder	2 Tbsp
Garlic	1 Tbsp, finely chopped
Annatto seed oil (see pg 78)	2 Tbsp
Salt	1/2 tsp
Sugar	1/2 Tbsp
Cooking oil	1 Tbsp
Lemon grass (*serai*)	2–3 stalks, bulbous portions only, bruised
Cinnamon stick	1, about 5-cm
Star anise	2
Carrots	2, cut into large chunks

DIPPING SAUCE

Red chilli	1, finely chopped
Lime juice	from 1 lime
Salt	1 tsp

METHOD

- Marinade beef with curry powder, 1/2 Tbsp garlic, 1 Tbsp annatto seed oil, salt and sugar for 30 minutes.
- Combine dipping sauce ingredients and set aside.
- Heat oil and stir-fry remaining garlic until fragrant. Add lemon grass, cinnamon, star anise and remaining annatto seed oil. Stir-fry for 2 minutes.
- Add beef and stir-fry for another 5 minutes. Pour in enough water to submerge beef. Bring to the boil then reduce heat and simmer for about 1 hour.
- When meat is 80 per cent tender, add carrots and cook until soft.
- Serve with dipping sauce and French baguette on the side.

Tip:
- *For the best results, do not cook the beef for too long or it will be too tender.*

GRILLED BEEF IN POINTED PEPPER LEAVES
(BO NUONG LA LOT)

Cooking time: 30 min   Serves 4

INGREDIENTS

Pointed pepper leaves (*daun kaduk*)	20, washed and drained
Cooking oil	
Chopped peanuts (groundnuts)	1 Tbsp
Mixed fish sauce (see pg 78) or fermented anchovy dip (see pg 78)	
Bamboo skewers	5

GRILLED BEEF

Minced beef	300 g
Garlic	1 tsp, finely chopped
Shallot	1 tsp, finely chopped
Salt	1/4 tsp
Sugar	1 tsp
Ground white pepper	1/2 tsp
Curry powder	1 tsp
Fried shallots	1 tsp
Cooking oil	1 tsp

METHOD

- Combine all grilled beef ingredients and mix well. Leave to marinade for 30 minutes.
- Lay a pointed pepper leaf flat on a plate and scoop 1 Tbsp of marinated beef onto it. Roll leaf up to form a small parcel about 5 cm long. Make 20 parcels.
- Skewer 4 parcels on each bamboo skewer. Brush parcels with some oil and grill until leaves are slightly charred.
- Sprinkle beef with ground peanuts then dip in mixed fish sauce or fermented anchovy dip before eating.

From left: Spiced Beef Stew with Baguette; Grilled Beef in Pointed Pepper Leaves

49

BEEF IN VINEGAR HOT POT (BO NHUNG DAM)

Cooking time: 20 min   Serves 4

INGREDIENTS

Beef tenderloin	500 g, thinly sliced
Onion	$1/2$, peeled and sliced
Spring onion (scallion)	1, sliced
Vietnamese rice paper	20 sheets, sprinkled with water to soften

HOT POT

Rice vinegar	250 ml
Lemon grass (*serai*)	2 Tbsp, bulbous portion only, finely sliced
Pineapple	300 g, peeled and sliced
Onion	1, peeled and finely sliced
Fresh coconut juice	250 ml
Salt	$1/2$ tsp
Sugar	2 tsp

SAUCE

Fermented anchovy sauce (see pg 78)	2 Tbsp
Water	125 ml
Pineapple	300 g, peeled and crushed
Garlic	2 cloves, peeled and crushed
Red chilli	1, finely chopped
Sugar	2 Tbsp

GARNISH

Lettuce	100 g
Mint leaves	3–4 sprigs
Cucumber	1, peeled and sliced
Pickled carrot and radish (see pg 79)	150 g
Fresh rice vermicelli (*beehoon*)	50 g, blanched

METHOD

- Prepare garnish ingredients and set aside.
- Combine sauce ingredients and set aside.
- Combine hot pot ingredients in a pot and bring to the boil. Reduce heat and simmer for 5 minutes.
- Lay slices of beef out on a plate and top with sliced onion and spring onion. Allow guests to dip slices of beef into the simmering hot pot to cook until their desired doneness.
- To assemble, lay a sheet of rice paper on a plate and arrange some garnish on it. Top with cooked beef and wrap. Dip in sauce before eating.

SAUTÉED FROG LEGS WITH LEMON GRASS (ECH XAO SA OT)

Cooking time: 20 min   Serves 4

INGREDIENTS

Frog legs	300 g, cleaned
Lemon grass (*serai*)	1 Tbsp, bulbous portion only, finely chopped
Red chilli	1, finely chopped
Salt	$1/4$ tsp
Sugar	$1/2$ tsp
Cooking oil	2 Tbsp
Garlic	1 tsp, finely chopped

METHOD

- Marinate frog legs with $1/2$ Tbsp lemon grass, half the chilli, salt and sugar.
- Heat cooking oil and stir-fry garlic until golden brown. Add remaining lemon grass and remaining chilli. Stir-fry until fragrant.
- Add frog legs and stir-fry until cooked. Season to taste with more salt if necessary. Serve with steamed rice.

Anti-clockwise from left: Beef in Vinegar Hot Pot; Beef Rolls; Steamed Rice; Sautéed Frog Legs with Lemon Grass

SIMMERED RIVER PRAWNS (TOM CANG RIM)

Cooking time: 30 min   Serves 4

INGREDIENTS

Freshwater prawns (shrimps)	500 g (6–8 pieces), deveined
Salt	1 tsp
Black peppercorns	1 tsp, cracked
Cooking oil	2 Tbsp
Sugar	2 Tbsp
Garlic	1 tsp, finely chopped
Fish sauce	1 Tbsp
Onion	1, peeled and cut into wedges
Water	125 ml

METHOD

- Marinade prawns with salt and $1/4$ tsp pepper for 15 minutes.
- Heat oil and add sugar and garlic. Cook until garlic turns golden brown and sugar caramelises.
- Add prawns and mix well. Reduce heat and simmer, flipping prawns over frequently.
- Add fish sauce, onion, remaining pepper and water. Cook uncovered for 10 minutes until prawns are completely cooked.
- Remove prawns but leave sauce to cook further. Allow it to reduce until slightly sticky. Pour over prawns.

Tip:
- *If freshwater prawns are not available, use tiger prawns or any other type of prawn.*

SNAILS STUFFED WITH MINCED PORK (OC BUOU NHOI THIT)

Cooking time: 1 hr   Serves 4

INGREDIENTS

Snails	2 kg, about 12 pieces, cleaned
Minced pork	100 g
Wood ear fungus	25 g, soaked to soften and finely chopped
Shallot	1 Tbsp, finely chopped
Garlic	1 tsp, finely chopped
Ginger	1 tsp, finely chopped
Salt	$1/2$ tsp
Ground white pepper	$1/2$ tsp
Sugar	$1/2$ tsp
Lemon grass (*serai*)	12 stalks or 12 ginger leaves

DIPPING SAUCE

Fish sauce	1 Tbsp
Water	2 Tbsp
Sugar	2 tsp
Ginger	1.5-cm knob, peeled and crushed

METHOD

- Boil snails for 5 minutes then shell, clean and mince. Reserve shells.
- Mix minced snails with minced pork, wood ear fungus, shallot, garlic, ginger, salt, pepper and sugar.
- Insert a small length of lemon grass or a ginger leaf into snail shells. Stuff meat mixture into shells and steam for 10 minutes over high heat.
- Combine dipping sauce ingredients and serve on the side with steamed snails.

Chef's Note:
- *You can use either sea or pond snails in this recipe.*

From top: Simmered River Prawns; Snails Stuffed with Minced Pork

CRISPY SOFT SHELL CRABS
(CUA LOT CHIEN GION)

Cooking time: 30 min   Serves 4

INGREDIENTS

Cooking oil for deep-frying	
Soft shell crabs	8, cleaned and each cut in half
Butter	1 Tbsp
Chilli sauce	2 Tbsp
Mayonnaise	2 Tbsp

BATTER

Rice flour	150 g
Plain (all-purpose) flour	100 g
Corn flour (cornstarch)	40 g
Egg yolk	1
Egg	1
Salt	1/2 tsp
Ground white pepper	1/2 tsp
Water	200 ml

METHOD

- Combine all batter ingredients except water in a large bowl. Gradually add water into batter, mixing well after each addition to get a thick batter.
- Heat oil for deep-frying in a large wok.
- Dip crabs into batter and coat well. Deep-fry until golden brown. Remove and drain well.
- In another wok, heat butter and toss in crabs. Coat well with butter. Remove and arrange on a serving plate.
- Serve with chilli and mayonnaise.

Tip:

- *For a stronger garlic flavour, marinate the crabs with pepper and garlic juice for about 30 minutes before coating with batter.*

CRABS WITH TAMARIND SAUCE
(CUA RANG ME)

Cooking time: 1 hr   Serves 4

INGREDIENTS

Crabs	2, large
Tamarind (*asam*) pulp	2 Tbsp, mixed with 2 Tbsp warm water
Sugar	2 Tbsp
Salt	1/2 tsp
Ground white pepper	1/2 tsp
Annatto seed oil (see pg 78)	1 tsp
Cooking oil for deep-frying	
Garlic	4 cloves, peeled and finely chopped

METHOD

- Clean crabs. Pull top shells off crabs and remove feathery lungs. Rinse. Pull off triangular-shaped shell on the underside and rinse crab again. Twist off claws and crack. Cut crabs in half.
- Into a small bowl, add tamarind pulp, sugar, salt, pepper and annatto seed oil. Set aside.
- Heat oil in a large wok and deep-fry crabs until they turn red. Remove and discard oil.
- In the same wok, heat another 2 Tbsp oil and stir-fry garlic until fragrant.
- Add crabs and tamarind mixture and cook until sauce is thick. Serve with steamed rice.

Tip:

- *When deep-frying the crabs, ensure that the oil is very hot. The crab meat will then be firm and tasty.*

From top: Crispy Soft Shell Crabs; Crabs with Tamarind Sauce

FISH STEAMED WITH SOY BEANS (CA CHUNG TUONG)

Cooking time: 30 min   Serves 4

INGREDIENTS

Sea bass	1, about 500 g, cleaned
Salt	1/4 tsp
Ground white pepper	1/2 tsp
Pork	100 g, thinly sliced
Spring onion (scallion)	1, cut into 2.5-cm lengths
Ginger	2.5-cm knob, peeled and julienned
Onion	1/2, large, peeled and sliced
Preserved soy beans (*taucheo*)	2 Tbsp
Light soy sauce	1 Tbsp
Red chillies	2, julienned
Sugar	1 tsp
Water or stock	250 ml

METHOD

- Make diagonal cuts on both sides of fish. Marinate with salt and 1/4 tsp pepper and leave for 15 minutes.
- Mix pork with spring onion, ginger, onion, preserved soy beans, light soy sauce, chillies, sugar, remaining pepper and water or stock. Place on top of fish.
- Steam for 15 minutes or until fish is cooked. Serve hot with steamed rice.

Tip:

- *You can also use any white fish fillet if you prefer not to use a whole fish for this recipe.*

FRIED FISH WITH LEMON GRASS AND CHILLI (CA CHIEN SA OT)

Cooking time: 20 min   Serves 4

INGREDIENTS

Lemon grass (*serai*)	2 stalks, bulbous portions only, thinly sliced then minced
Garlic	3 cloves, peeled and finely chopped
Red chillies	2, finely chopped
Fish sauce	2 Tbsp
Sugar	1/2 tsp
Ground turmeric	1/2 tsp
White fish fillet or 1 red snapper	500 g
Cooking oil for deep-frying	

DIPPING SAUCE

Fish sauce	
Red chilli	1, finely chopped

METHOD

- Combine lemon grass, garlic, chillies, fish sauce, sugar and ground turmeric.
- Coat fish with mixture and leave to marinate for 15 minutes.
- Heat cooking oil and deep-fry fish on one side until golden brown before turning over to cook the other side.
- Remove and drain well. Serve with steamed rice and a dipping sauce of fish sauce and chopped chilli.

From top: Fish Steamed with Soy Beans; Fried Fish with Lemon Grass and Chilli

SIMMERED FISH (CA KHO TO)

Cooking time: 30 min   Serves 4

INGREDIENTS

Mud fish or any fish fillet	500 g, cleaned
Fish sauce	1 Tbsp
Sugar	1 tsp
Caramel syrup (see pg 78)	1 tsp
Chicken seasoning powder	1 tsp
Ground white pepper	1/4 tsp
Spring onion (scallion)	1, white portion only, chopped
Red chilli	1, chopped
Cooking oil	1 tsp
Water	4 Tbsp

GARNISH
Spring onion (scallion)

METHOD
- Cut fish into 100 g steaks. Marinate with fish sauce, sugar, caramel syrup, chicken seasoning powder and pepper for 15 minutes.
- Mash spring onion and chilli together using a mortar and pestle.
- Heat oil and stir-fry mashed spring onion and chilli mixture until fragrant.
- Add fish and cook each side for 5 minutes. Add water and simmer until sauce is thick and coats fish.
- Garnish with spring onion and sprinkle with pepper as desired. Serve with steamed rice.

Tip:
- *Use stock in place of water to simmer fish for an even richer flavour.*

PRAWNS AND PORK SIMMERED IN COCONUT JUICE (TEP RANG NUOC DUA)

Cooking time: 30 min   Serves 4

INGREDIENTS

Pork belly	200 g, thickly sliced
Ground white pepper	
Salt	
Cooking oil	1 Tbsp
Garlic	2 cloves, peeled and finely chopped
Sugar	1 Tbsp
Prawns (shrimps)	300 g
Fresh coconut juice	from 1 young coconut

METHOD
- Marinate pork with some pepper and salt.
- Heat oil and stir-fry garlic until fragrant. Add sugar and cook until it caramelises.
- Add pork and stir-fry until half-cooked. Add prawns and stir-fry until they turn red.
- Season with more salt and pepper to taste.
- Add coconut juice and bring to the boil then simmer until sauce is thick. Serve with steamed rice.

Tip:
- *If coconut juice is not available, use stock or water.*

From top: Simmered Fish; Prawns and Pork Simmered in Coconut Juice

STEAMED PRAWNS IN COCONUT JUICE (TOM HAP NUOC DUA)

Cooking time: 20 min   Serves 4

INGREDIENTS

Fresh coconut juice	from 1 young coconut, reserve coconut
Sugar	1 tsp
Tiger prawns (shrimps)	12
Vietnamese rice paper	10 sheets, sprinkled with water to soften
Dried fine rice vermicelli (*beehoon*)	25 g, soaked and steamed for 5 minutes
Chopped peanuts (groundnuts)	1 Tbsp
Seasoned lime juice (see pg 79)	

GARNISH

Lettuce, mint and sliced cucumber	
Pickled carrot and radish (see pg 79)	150 g

METHOD
- Boil coconut juice and sugar. Stir until sugar is melted.
- Add prawns and boil for 10 minutes until prawns turn red and are cooked. Drain and remove prawns.
- Pour juice back into coconut and hang prawns around coconut.
- Place on a serving plate with rice paper, rice vermicelli, peanuts, lettuce, mint leaves, cucumber and seasoned lime juice to serve.
- To assemble, lay a sheet of rice paper on a plate. Arrange lettuce, mint leaves, cucumber, pickled carrot and radish, rice vermicelli, peanuts and a peeled prawn on top. Roll up and dip into seasoned lime juice before eating.

STEAMED CRABS IN BEER BROTH (CUA HAP BIA)

Cooking time: 20 min   Serves 4

INGREDIENTS

Crabs	1 kg, about 2
Salt	$1/2$ tsp
Ground white pepper	$1/2$ tsp
Sugar	1 tsp
Beer	250 ml

GARNISH

Red chilli	1, julienned
Coriander (cilantro)	1 Tbsp
Spring onion (scallion)	1 Tbsp, julienned

METHOD
- Clean crabs. Pull top shells off crabs and remove feathery lungs. Rinse. Pull off triangular-shaped shell on the underside and rinse crab again. Twist off claws and crack. Cut crabs in half.
- Marinate crabs with salt, pepper and sugar in a heatproof (flameproof) bowl for 30 minutes.
- Pour in three-quarters of the beer then steam covered for 15 minutes. Pour in remaining beer, cover and leave for a few more minutes.
- Remove from heat and garnish with chilli, coriander and spring onion.

From left: Steamed Prawns in Coconut Juice; Steamed Crabs in Beer Broth

STUFFED SQUID (MUC NHOI THIT)

Cooking time: 1 hr   Serves 4

INGREDIENTS

Squid tubes	6, medium-sized, cleaned
Cooking oil for deep-frying	

STUFFING

Minced pork	300 g
Wood ear fungus	4, soaked to soften and finely chopped
Glass noodles (*tunghoon*)	25 g, soaked to soften, drained and cut into 2-cm lengths
Spring onion (scallion)	1 tsp, white portion only, finely chopped
Sugar	1 tsp
Salt	¼ tsp
Ground white pepper	¼ tsp

COATING

Eggs	2, beaten
Corn flour (cornstarch)	60 g

TOMATO SAUCE

Shallot	1 Tbsp, finely chopped
Tomatoes	4, peeled, seeded and finely chopped
Fish sauce	¼ Tbsp
Sugar	1 tsp
Salt	¼ tsp
Ground white pepper	¼ tsp

METHOD

- Combine stuffing ingredients and mix well.
- Stuff mixture into squid tubes and secure with toothpicks. Use another toothpick to create some small holes in squid tubes so they do not burst when steaming. Steam stuffed squid tubes for 15 minutes.
- Dip steamed squid in beaten egg then coat with corn flour.
- Heat oil for deep-frying in a wok then deep-fry squid until golden brown. Drain and set aside.
- Leave 1 Tbsp oil in wok and sauté shallot and tomatoes until fragrant and soft. Simmer for 10 minutes then season with fish sauce, sugar, salt and pepper.
- Remove toothpicks and slice squid into rounds. Serve with tomato sauce and steamed rice.

STEAMED SQUID WITH GINGER AND SPRING ONION (MUC HAP HANH GUNG)

Cooking time: 20 min   Serves 4

INGREDIENTS

Squid	500 g, cleaned
Ginger	2.5-cm knob, peeled and julienned
Spring onion (scallion)	1, cut into 3-cm lengths
Onion	½, peeled and sliced
Red chilli	1, julienned
Rice wine	1 Tbsp

SAUCE

Fish sauce	2 Tbsp
Sugar	2 Tbsp
Garlic	2 cloves, peeled and finely chopped
Red chilies	2, finely chopped
Lime juice	from 1 lime
Ginger	1.5-cm, peeled and finely chopped

METHOD

- Combine all sauce ingredients. Mix well and set aside.
- Slit open squid tubes and flatten. Make diagonal cuts on the inner surface then slice.
- Place squid on a deep heatproof (flameproof) plate and top with ginger, spring onion, onion and chilli. Pour rice wine over.
- Steam for 10 minutes. Serve hot with sauce on the side.

Chef's Note:

- *This dish can served as a starter or as part of a main meal with steamed rice.*

From left: Stuffed Squid; Steamed Squid with Ginger and Spring Onion

THANG LONG FISH CAKE
(CHA CA THANG LONG)

Cooking time: 1 hr   Serves 4

INGREDIENTS

Red snapper	1, about 1 kg, cleaned and cut into pieces
Galangal	2.5-cm knob, peeled and finely pounded
Turmeric powder	1 tsp
Fine prawn (shrimp) paste	1 tsp
Cooking oil	3 Tbsp
Ground white pepper	1 tsp
Spring onions (scallions)	2, white bulbous ends only
Dill	100 g or more as preferred
Fresh fine rice vermicelli (*beehoon*)	500 g, blanched

PRAWN PASTE SAUCE

Fine prawn (shrimp) paste	1 tsp
Lime juice	2 Tbsp
Sugar	1 tsp
Red chilli	1, finely chopped

GARNISH

Lettuce, mint, chopped peanuts (groundnuts)

METHOD

- Combine fish, galangal, turmeric powder, prawn paste, 1 Tbsp cooking oil and pepper. Mix well and set aside for 30 minutes.
- Combine all prawn paste sauce ingredients except chilli and mix well. Mix in chopped chilli. Set aside.
- On a charcoal grill or oven, grill fish until golden brown on both sides.
- In a wok, heat remaining cooking oil, add spring onions, grilled fish and dill.
- Divide rice vermicelli equally into 4 serving bowls, then top with some lettuce, mint, fish, dill and peanuts. Mix with some prawn paste sauce before eating.

CRABS IN GARLIC AND PEPPER SALT
(CUA RANG MUOI)

Cooking time: 30 min   Serves 4

INGREDIENTS

Crabs	2, about 1.5 kg
Cooking oil for deep-frying	
Garlic	1 Tbsp, finely chopped
Annatto seed oil (see pg 78)	$1/2$ tsp
Spring onion (scallion)	1 tsp, finely chopped
Chicken stock or water	125 ml
Salt	$1/2$ tsp
Sugar	1 tsp
Ground white pepper	$1/2$ tsp

METHOD

- Clean crabs. Pull top shells off crabs and remove feathery lungs. Rinse. Pull off triangular-shaped shell on the underside and rinse crab again. Twist off claws and crack. Cut crabs in half.
- Heat oil in a wok and deep-fry crabs over high heat for 10 minutes. Remove and drain well.
- Leaving 1 Tbsp oil in the wok, stir-fry garlic until fragrant then return crabs to wok and stir-fry for about 5 minutes.
- Add remaining ingredients and stir-fry for a few more minutes until crabs are well-coated in sauce. Remove from heat and serve.

From left: Thang Long Fish Cake; Crabs in Garlic and Pepper Salt

DEEP-FRIED PRAWNS COATED WITH SESAME SEEDS (TOM LAN ME)

Cooking time: 20 min   Serves 4

INGREDIENTS

Tiger prawns (shrimps)	500 g, peeled and deveined
Salt	$1/4$ tsp
Ground white pepper	$1/4$ tsp
White sesame seeds	150 g
Cooking oil for deep-frying	

BATTER

Egg	1, beaten
Plain (all-purpose) flour	100 g
Tapioca flour	50 g
Salt	$1/2$ tsp
Ground white pepper	$1/2$ tsp
Annatto seed oil (see pg 78)	$1/2$ tsp
Cold water	

PINEAPPLE SAUCE

Pineapple	300 g, peeled, sliced and finely blended
Water	125 ml
Sugar	1 Tbsp
Salt	$1/2$ tsp
Corn flour (cornstarch)	2 tsp, mixed with 1 Tbsp water

METHOD

- Wash prawns with lightly salted water then butterfly them by cutting a slit through the back.
- Marinate prawns with salt and pepper for 10 minutes.
- Combine batter ingredients with just enough cold water to form a paste.
- Dip prawns in batter then coat with sesame seeds.
- Heat oil for deep-frying on medium heat. Deep-fry prawns until golden brown. Drain well.
- Combine all pineapple sauce ingredients except corn flour and bring to the boil. Simmer for 5 minutes then thicken with corn flour mixture.
- Serve prawns with pineapple sauce as a dip.

FRIED MACKEREL WITH FISH SAUCE (CA THU CHIEN SOT CA)

Cooking time: 15 min   Serves 2

INGREDIENTS

Mackerel	1, about 300 g, cleaned and cut into steaks
Cooking oil for deep-frying	
Garlic	1 tsp, finely chopped
Onion	$1/4$, peeled and finely chopped
Tomatoes	2, finely chopped
Salt	$1/4$ tsp
Fish sauce	1 Tbsp
Chicken seasoning powder	1 tsp
Sugar	$1/4$ tsp
Ground white pepper	$1/4$ tsp

METHOD

- Dry fish steaks thoroughly.
- Heat oil for deep-frying and fry fish until golden brown on both sides. Drain and set aside.
- In a clean wok, heat 1 Tbsp oil and stir-fry garlic and onion until fragrant.
- Add tomatoes and cook for 5 minutes. Add salt.
- Stir in fish sauce, chicken seasoning powder, sugar, pepper and more salt if necessary.
- Pour tomato sauce over fish and serve with steamed rice.

Tip:

- *To make a finer tomato sauce, remove the skin of the tomatoes. You can do this by first cutting a cross at the bottom of the tomatoes and then placing them in boiling water for 10 seconds. Drain then place tomatoes into a bowl of iced water. This will make it easier to peel the skin off.*

From top: Deep-fried Prawns Coated with Sesame Seeds; Fried Mackerel with Fish Sauce

CRISPY SQUID
(MUC CHIEN GION)

Cooking time: 30 min Serves 4

INGREDIENTS

Squid	500 g, cleaned
Rice vinegar	2 Tbsp
Water	500 ml
Ground white pepper	1/4 tsp
Salt	1 tsp
Cooking oil for deep-frying	
Mayonnaise	
Chilli sauce	

BATTER

Egg	1, well-beaten
Plain (all-purpose) flour	100 g
Tapioca flour	50 g
Cold water	
Cooking oil	1 Tbsp
Salt	1/2 tsp
Ground white pepper	1/2 tsp
Annatto seed oil (see pg 78)	1 tsp

GARNISH

Lettuce and sliced cucumber

METHOD

- Score squid tubes with criss-cross cuts then cut into bite-sized pieces.
- Bring vinegar and water to the boil. Blanch squid, then drain well.
- Marinate squid with pepper and salt.
- Combine batter ingredients.
- Heat oil for deep-frying. Dip squid in batter then deep-fry in hot oil until golden brown.
- Serve with mayonnaise, chilli sauce, lettuce and sliced cucumber.

RICE WRAPPED IN LOTUS LEAF
(COM HOANG BAO)

Cooking time: 30 min Serves 2–4

INGREDIENTS

Cooking oil	1 Tbsp
Prawns (shrimps)	200 g, cooked, peeled and diced
Carrots	100 g, diced and boiled until soft
Dried Chinese mushrooms	4, soaked to soften then drained and diced
Ham	100 g, diced
Dried lotus seeds	50 g, bitter embryos removed and boiled until soft
Rice	200 g, washed and cooked
Salt	1/2 tsp
Ground white pepper	1/4 tsp
Sugar	1/4 tsp
Chicken seasoning powder	1/4 tsp
Lotus leaf	1, large

METHOD

- Heat oil in a wok and stir-fry prawns, carrots, mushrooms, ham and lotus seeds for 5 minutes.
- Add cooked rice and stir-fry for another 10 minutes. Mix in salt, pepper, sugar and chicken seasoning powder.
- Scoop rice into a bowl and turn rice over onto lotus leaf. Bring 2 opposite edges of lotus leaf up to enclose rice, then tuck the other 2 edges underneath parcel.
- Place in a steamer to cook for 10 minutes.
- Carefully transfer lotus leaf parcel onto a plate and cut open to reveal rice. Serve hot.

Tip:

- *Since the lotus seeds have already been cooked by boiling, you can choose to display them on top of the rice just before serving as shown here, instead of adding them in when frying the rice.*

From top: Rice Wrapped in Lotus Leaf; Crispy Squid

CHICKEN PORRIDGE
(CHAO GA)

Cooking time: 2 hr   Serves 10

INGREDIENTS

Whole chicken	1, about 1.5 kg, cleaned
Rice	200 g
Glutinous rice	50 g
Fish sauce	3 Tbsp
Sugar	1 tsp
Chicken seasoning powder	1 Tbsp
Ground white pepper	1 tsp

GARNISH

Spring onions (scallions)	2, thinly sliced
Polygonum (*laksa*) leaves (*daun kesum*)	3–4 sprigs, finely chopped

METHOD

- In a deep pot, pour in just enough water to submerge chicken and bring to the boil. Place chicken in and boil for 30 minutes until well-cooked. Remove chicken and reserve stock.
- Plunge chicken into cold water and leave until slightly cooled. Shred meat and set aside. Discard chicken carcass.
- Place rice and glutinous rice in reserved stock. Bring to the boil then lower heat and simmer, stirring constantly. Cook until rice is very soft and mixture is thick.
- Add fish sauce, sugar and chicken seasoning powder.
- To serve, ladle porridge into individual serving bowls. Top with shredded chicken and garnish with spring onion and polygonum leaves. Sprinkle with pepper.

Tip:

- *Instead of discarding the chicken gizzard and liver when cleaning the chicken, you can also serve them with the porridge. Wash and rinse thoroughly then drain and slice into small pieces. Heat some oil and sauté 1 chopped shallot until fragrant. Add chicken gizzard and liver and season with 1 tsp fish sauce. Add to porridge before serving.*

VIETNAMESE FRIED RICE
(COM CHIEN)

Cooking time: 30 min   Serves 4

INGREDIENTS

Rice	300 g
Carrot	40 g, diced
Prawns (shrimps)	200 g, deveined
Cooking oil	2 Tbsp
Eggs	2, lightly beaten
Garlic	2 cloves, peeled and finely chopped
Shallots	2, peeled and finely chopped
Chinese sausages	100 g, diced
Green peas	12 g
Salt	1/4 tsp
Sugar	1/2 tsp
Chicken seasoning powder	1 tsp
Ground white pepper	1/3 tsp
Spring onion (scallion)	1, thinly sliced

GARNISH

Coriander (cilantro)	1 sprig
Fish sauce	1 Tbsp
Red chilli	1, sliced

METHOD

- Wash and cook rice. Set cooked rice aside for it to cool completely.
- Blanch diced carrot in boiling water for 2 minutes. Drain well.
- Blanch prawns in boiling water. Drain well, peel and dice.
- Heat 1/2 Tbsp oil in a wok over medium heat. Add eggs, stirring quickly until cooked, then set aside.
- Reheat wok and add remaining oil. Sauté garlic and shallots until fragrant.
- Add prawns, Chinese sausages and carrot. Stir-fry for 5 minutes then add rice and green peas. Mix well.
- Season with salt, sugar, chicken seasoning powder and pepper. Mix in eggs and continue to fry for another 5 minutes or until rice is dry.
- Mix well for another few minutes until ingredients are well combined. Sprinkle in spring onion.
- Garnish with coriander and serve with fish sauce and sliced chilli.

From top: Chicken Porridge; Vietnamese Fried Rice

VIETNAMESE BO BO CHA CHA (CHE THUNG)

Cooking time: 1 hr   Serves 4

INGREDIENTS

Sweet potatoes	200 g, peeled, diced and soaked for 5 minutes
Tapioca	200 g, peeled, diced and soaked in lightly salted water for 10 minutes
Water	2 litres
Screwpine (*pandan*) leaves	50 g
Split green beans	200 g, soaked overnight
Peanuts (groundnuts)	100 g, soaked for 30 minutes then boiled until soft
Sago	20 g, soaked for 10 minutes
Wood ear fungus	10 g, soaked to soften and thinly sliced
Sugar	300 g
Coconut milk	250 ml
Vanilla powder	$1/2$ tsp

METHOD

- Drain sweet potatoes then boil or steam until cooked and soft.
- Drain tapioca then boil or steam until cooked and soft.
- Bring water to the boil with screwpine leaves. Add green beans and cook stirring until green beans are soft.
- Remove and discard screwpine leaves. Add sweet potatoes, tapioca, peanuts, sago and wood ear fungus and return to the boil.
- Add sugar then stir in coconut milk and vanilla powder. Serve warm.

CARAMEL CUSTARD (BANH FLAN)

Cooking time: 30 min   Serves 4–6

INGREDIENTS

Eggs	4, large
Sugar	300 g
Fresh milk	500 ml
Vanilla powder	$1/4$ tsp
Water	120 ml
Shaved ice	

METHOD

- In a large mixing bowl, beat eggs well with 100 g sugar, fresh milk and vanilla powder. Set aside.
- Into a pan, add half the water and the remaining sugar and bring to the boil. Stir well until sugar melts and syrup is a caramel colour.
- Add remaining water and stir well. Remove from heat. Pour 1 Tbsp of syrup each into 12 plastic or stainless steel moulds.
- Fill moulds up with beaten egg mixture. Arrange moulds in a steamer and steam for 30 minutes. To test if custard is cooked, simply insert a bamboo skewer into custard. If the skewer comes out clean, the custard is cooked.
- Remove from heat and leave to cool. Refrigerate until firm.
- To serve, use the tip of a small knife to go around inside edge of each mould. Then turn custard out onto dessert plates. Top with a shaved ice.

Tips:

- *You can give the custard a coffee flavour by adding a thin layer of thick coffee between the caramel and egg mixture before steaming.*
- *Steam on a lower setting to ensure a smooth custard.*

From top: Vietnamese Bo Bo Cha Cha; Caramel Custard

LOTUS SEEDS WITH AGAR-AGAR (CHE SEN THACH)

Cooking time: 1 hr   Serves 4

INGREDIENTS

Lotus seeds	300 g, soaked overnight to soften
Water	500 ml
Rock sugar	300 g
Vanilla powder	1/4 tsp

AGAR-AGAR

Agar-agar powder	30 g
Water	500 ml

METHOD

- Drain lotus seeds. Remove and discard the bitter embryos in the centre of the seeds with a toothpick. Rinse lotus seeds.
- Bring water to the boil with rock sugar until sugar is completed melted.
- Add lotus seeds and cook for another 5 minutes. Remove from heat and leave to cool. Stir in vanilla powder.
- Stir agar-agar powder into water then bring to the boil for 10 minutes. Pour into a container then leave to cool before chilling in the refrigerator.
- When agar-agar is completely set, cut into thin strips. Put agar-agar into lotus seed soup.
- Ladle into individual bowls and serve topped with shaved ice.

GREEN BEAN PASTE WITH COCONUT MILK (CHE DAU XANH DANH)

Cooking time: 1 hr   Serves 4

INGREDIENTS

Split green beans	500 g, soaked overnight
Water	2.1 litres
Sugar	300 g
Shaved ice	

COCONUT MILK SYRUP

Water	500 ml
Screwpine (*pandan*) leaves	100 g
Sugar	4 Tbsp
Coconut milk	6 Tbsp
Tapioca flour	1 Tbsp, mixed with 125 ml water

METHOD

- Drain green beans and boil in 2 litres water until soft. Alternatively, steam green beans until soft.
- Blend (process) green beans well with sugar and 100 ml water to mix well into a paste. Set aside to cool.
- Prepare coconut milk syrup. In a small pot, bring to the boil water and screwpine leaves for 10 minutes. Remove and discard screwpine leaves.
- Lower heat to a simmer then stir in sugar and coconut milk. Gradually add in tapioca flour mixture and stir until thick.
- Serve green bean paste in a glass topped with shaved ice and coconut milk syrup.

From left: Lotus Seeds with Agar-agar; Green Bean Paste with Coconut Milk

GLUTINOUS RICE BALLS (CHE TROI NUOC)

Cooking time: 1 hr   Serves 4

INGREDIENTS

Glutinous rice flour	500 g
Salt	1 1/2 tsp
Warm water	
Split green beans	200 g, soaked for 2 hours
Sugar	300 g
Ginger	50 g, peeled and chopped

TOPPING

Coconut milk syrup (see pg 74)	
White sesame seeds	20 g, toasted

METHOD

- In a large bowl, combine glutinous rice flour and 1 tsp salt. Gradually add enough warm water to form a soft pliable dough. Form the mixture into 3-cm balls.
- Steam green beans until soft then blend (process) into a paste. Stir-fry over low heat with remaining salt, 100 g sugar and 10 g chopped ginger. Stir-fry until bean paste is dry.
- Form mixture into balls, slightly smaller than the glutinous rice flour balls.
- Flatten a glutinous rice flour ball and press a bean paste ball into it. Roll to enclose green bean paste fully. Repeat with remaining glutinous rice flour balls and bean paste balls.
- Bring 2 litres water to the boil then add balls in to cook. When balls float to the surface, remove then rinse under running water for 2 minutes.
- Bring another 2 litres water to the boil then add in remaining sugar and ginger. Stir for 10 minutes.
- Place glutinous rice balls in and return to the boil.
- Serve glutinous rice balls with sugar syrup in a small bowl, topped with coconut milk syrup and sesame seeds.

BANANA SAGO (CHE CHUOI CHUNG)

Cooking time: 30 min   Serves 4

INGREDIENTS

Ripe bananas	8, peeled
Sugar	200 g
Salt	1/4 tsp
Coconut milk	500 ml
Water	250 ml
Screwpine (*pandan*) leaves	5, washed and tied into a knot
Sago	100 g, soaked for 2 hours

TOPPING

Ground, roasted peanuts (groundnuts) or toasted sesame seeds

METHOD

- Sprinkle bananas with some sugar and salt.
- Combine half the coconut milk, water, remaining sugar and salt and screwpine leaves in a saucepan. Cook over medium heat for 10 minutes, stirring often.
- Add bananas and sago. When bananas are well-cooked, add remaining coconut milk and remove from heat.
- Allow to cool then serve sprinkled with peanuts or sesame seeds.

From top: Glutinous Rice Balls; Banana Sago

Basic Recipes

Annatto Seed Oil (*Mau Dieu*)

INGREDIENTS

Cooking oil	3 Tbsp
Annatto seeds	2 Tbsp

METHOD

- Heat oil and stir-fry annatto seeds until oil turns a light reddish colour. Strain oil and discard seeds.

Bean Paste Dip

INGREDIENTS

Water	250 ml
Glutinous rice	10 g, soaked for 1 hour
Split green beans	10 g, soaked overnight
Pork or chicken liver	10 g, sliced
Preserved soy beans (*taucheo*)	1/2 Tbsp
Sugar	1/2 tsp
Salt	1/8 tsp

METHOD

- Bring water, glutinous rice and green beans to the boil until soft and fine like porridge.
- Blend together with liver and preserved soy beans until smooth.
- Bring to the boil and season with sugar and salt. Serve as a dipping sauce.

Caramel Syrup (*Nuoc Mau*)

INGREDIENTS

Water	250 ml
White or brown sugar	200 g

METHOD

- Bring water and sugar to the boil, stirring. Reduce heat and simmer until liquid is dark brown in colour.
- Remove from heat and add in 2–3 Tbsp water and stir.
- Pour into a glass container and cover. Use as required.

Fermented Anchovy Dip (*Mam Nem*)

INGREDIENTS

Fermented anchovy paste	2 Tbsp
Pineapple	2 Tbsp, finely crushed
Garlic	1 clove, peeled and finely chopped
Red chilli	1, seeded and finely chopped
Lemon grass (*serai*)	1 stalk, bulbous portion only, finely chopped
Sugar	1 tsp
Water	125 ml

METHOD

- Combine ingredients and mix well. Bring to the boil stirring then allow to cool. Serve as a dipping sauce.

Mixed Fish Sauce (*Nuoc Mam Pha*)

INGREDIENTS

Water	60 ml
Rice vinegar	1 tsp
Sugar	2 tsp
Red chilli	1, seeded, and finely chopped
Garlic	2 cloves, peeled and crushed
Lime juice	1 tsp
Fish sauce	2 Tbsp

METHOD

- Mix ingredients together and serve as a dipping sauce.
- If making in larger amounts however, bring water, vinegar and sugar to the boil then allow to cool before adding chilli, garlic and lime juice. Stir in fish sauce before serving.

Peanut Sauce (*Tuong Dau Phong*)

INGREDIENTS

Water	3 Tbsp
Peanut butter	1 Tbsp
Hoisin sauce	2 tsp
Corn flour (cornstarch)	1 tsp, mixed with 1 Tbsp water
Red chilli	1, seeded and finely chopped
Chopped peanuts (groundnuts)	1 tsp

METHOD
- Combine water, peanut butter and hoisin sauce and bring to the boil.
- Add corn flour mixture and stir until sauce is thick.
- Serve topped with chopped chilli and peanuts.

Pickled Carrot

INGREDIENTS

Sugar	2 Tbsp
Rice vinegar	1 Tbsp
Water	1 litre
Carrot	100 g, julienned

METHOD
- Combine sugar, vinegar and water then add carrot and leave for at least 2 hours. Drain then serve as a side dish.

Pickled Carrot and Radish

INGREDIENTS

Sugar	2 Tbsp
Rice vinegar	1 Tbsp
Water	1 litre
Carrot	50 g, julienned
Radish	50 g, julienned

METHOD
- Combine sugar, vinegar and water then add carrot and radish and leave for at least 2 hours. Drain then serve as a side dish.

Salad Dressing (*Nuoc Goi*)

INGREDIENTS

Lime juice	2 Tbsp
Fish sauce	1 Tbsp
Red chilli	1, seeded and finely chopped
Garlic	2 cloves, peeled and finely chopped
Sugar	2 Tbsp
Salt	$1/2$ tsp

METHOD
- Combine all ingredients and mix well.

Seasoned Lime Juice (*Muoi Tieu Chanh*)

INGREDIENTS

Lime juice	1 Tbsp
Salt	1 tsp
Ground white pepper	1 Tbsp

METHOD
- Combine ingredients and mix well. Use as a dipping sauce.

GLOSSARY

Red Fermented Bean Curd
These small pieces of bean curd have a very pungent flavour. They have a thick cheesy consistency and is commonly used to flavour meat dishes.

Fermented Anchovy Sauce
This strong-smelling sauce is opaque brown in colour and thicker than regular fish sauce. It is made from fermenting anchovies into a paste. The Vietnamese love it, but those who are not accustomed to its strong flavour can stick to the milder fish sauce.

Fish Sauce
This clear dark brown sauce is made by fermenting anchovies in salt and collecting the resulting juices. It is commonly used as a seasoning when cooking as well a table condiment in Vietnam. Quality varies and the best fish sauce is light in colour and clear.

Hoisin Sauce
This thick dark sauce is sweet and is used mainly as a dip, whether on its own or mixed with other sauces, in Vietnam. In Chinese cooking, it is used in stir-fries.

Preserved Soy Beans (*Taucheo*)
Also known as yellow bean sauce, this brown-coloured sauce is made by cooking then fermenting soy beans in salt and spices. It is available in cans or jars, with the beans whole or mashed.

Rice Vinegar
This clear white vinegar is relatively mild compared to western vinegars. It is used as a pickling agent for Vietnamese pickles.

Ginger Leaves
These are the long slender leaves of the ginger plant. They are commonly used whole to flavour meat dishes. Some recipes also require that they be finely sliced and added.

Pointed Pepper Leaves (*Daun Kaduk*)
Also known as wild betel leaves, these broad leaves are used as food wrappers in Vietnam. Thus cooked, the leaves impart a lovely aroma to the dish.

Polygonum (*Laksa*) Leaves (*Daun Kesum*)
Also known as Vietnamese mint, polygonum leaves have a pleasant and distinctive fragrance. The Vietnamese consume a large amount of fresh greens, and this is one of them. It is commonly eaten in salads or spring rolls.

Thai Parsley
These long jagged edges leaves have a similar flavour to coriander or Chinese parsley, hence its name. It is another herb that the Vietnamese use in their salads and spring rolls.

Mint Leaves
With a refreshing minty fragrance, mint leaves are commonly eaten whole and fresh in salads or spring rolls in Vietnam.

Thai Basil Leaves
Easily recognisable from their deep purple stems and flowers, Thai basil has a mild flavour and makes up another of the greens that the Vietnamese favour with their salads and spring rolls.

GLOSSARY

Lotus Seeds
These are the dried seeds of the freshwater lotus plant. They are enjoyed in both sweet and savoury dishes. Soak overnight to soften then remove the bitter embryos before cooking.

Rice Vermicelli (*Beehoon*)
Rice vermicelli is available fresh or dried, although the dried form is more commonly available. To reconstitute, simply soak in warm water to soften before using. There are various sizes of rice vermicelli—thick and round, fine and round, and flat. In Vietnamese cooking, rice vermicelli is commonly used in soups, spring rolls and salads.

Glass Noodles (*Tunghoon*)
Also known as cellophane noodles, these fine noodles are made from mung bean flour and have no flavour of their own. Hence, they readily absorb the flavour of the soup or stock they are cooked or served in. Soak in warm water to soften before using.

Annatto Seeds
These are the small red seeds of a tropical plant. They are commonly used as a food dye or to flavour oils. The seeds are then discarded, not consumed.

Sago
These small balls of starch are made from the sago palm. They can be used as thickeners, but are more commonly enjoyed in desserts in Vietnam. When boiled, they become translucent.

Split Green Beans
These are dried green beans that have been skinned and split. They are very versatile and can be used in both sweet and savoury dishes.

Turmeric Powder
This powder is ground from the dried turmeric root. It is commonly added to dishes to impart a rich yellow colour, not unlike saffron. Be very careful when using turmeric powder though, as it stains.

Sweet Potatoes
There are a few varieties of sweet potatoes and this is the purplish coloured variety. It is sweet in flavour and is commonly used in sweet desserts. Store in a cool, dark place.

Green Bananas
These are unripe bananas which cannot be eaten raw as a fruit. When they are steamed however, they are soft and delicious.

Banana Bud
The unopened bud of the banana flower has tough outer layers that are sometimes used as disposable but pretty food containers. To get to the edible yellow part, these tough outer layers must first be removed.

Tapioca
The tapioca is a tuber and has rough brown skin. It is white inside and when cooked, it remains rather fibrous. Store in a cool, dark place.

Lotus Stems
These are the stems of young lotus plants. These slender stems have a crisp, crunchy texture and are used in Vietnamese salads.

WEIGHTS & MEASURES

Quantities for this book are given in metric measures.
Standard measurements used are: 1 tsp = 5 ml, 1 Tbsp = 15 ml, 1 cup = 250 ml.
All measures are level unless otherwise stated.

LIQUID AND VOLUME MEASURES

Metric	Imperial	American
5 ml	1/6 fl oz	1 teaspoon
10 ml	1/3 fl oz	1 dessertspoon
15 ml	1/2 fl oz	1 tablespoon
60 ml	2 fl oz	1/4 cup (4 tablespoons)
85 ml	2 1/2 fl oz	1/3 cup
90 ml	3 fl oz	3/8 cup (6 tablespoons)
125 ml	4 fl oz	1/2 cup
180 ml	6 fl oz	3/4 cup
250 ml	8 fl oz	1 cup
300 ml	10 fl oz (1/2 pint)	1 1/4 cups
375 ml	12 fl oz	1 1/2 cups
435 ml	14 fl oz	1 3/4 cups
500 ml	16 fl oz	2 cups
625 ml	20 fl oz (1 pint)	2 1/2 cups
750 ml	24 fl oz (1 1/5 pints)	3 cups
1 litre	32 fl oz (1 3/5 pints)	4 cups
1.25 litres	40 fl oz (2 pints)	5 cups
1.5 litres	48 fl oz (2 2/5 pints)	6 cups
2.5 litres	80 fl oz (4 pints)	10 cups

OVEN TEMPERATURE

Regulo	°C	°F	Gas
Very slow	120	250	1
Slow	150	300	2
Moderately slow	160	325	3
Moderate	180	350	4
Moderately hot	190/200	370/400	5/6
Hot	210/220	410/440	6/7
Very hot	230	450	8
Super hot	250/290	475/550	9/10

LENGTH

Metric	Imperial
0.5 cm	1/4 inch
1 cm	1/2 inch
1.5 cm	3/4 inch
2.5 cm	1 inch

DRY MEASURES

Metric	Imperial
30 grams	1 ounce
45 grams	1 1/2 ounces
55 grams	2 ounces
70 grams	2 1/2 ounces
85 grams	3 ounces
100 grams	3 1/2 ounces
110 grams	4 ounces
125 grams	4 1/2 ounces
140 grams	5 ounces
280 grams	10 ounces
450 grams	16 ounces (1 pound)
500 grams	1 pound, 1 1/2 ounces
700 grams	1 1/2 pounds
800 grams	1 3/4 pounds
1 kilogram	2 pounds, 3 ounces
1.5 kilograms	3 pounds, 4 1/2 ounces
2 kilograms	4 pounds, 6 ounces

ABBREVIATION

tsp	teaspoon
Tbsp	tablespoon
g	gram
kg	kilogram
ml	millilitre